Contents

Great America's Ideology

Trump's Warriors

Destroying Israel

Great America's Ideology

Trump's shockwave

The Trump Effect is a kind of sickness in the democratic system. The early symptoms—nativist grumblings, nocturnal tweeting, and disinhibited behavior around women and immigrants—may lead to a crisis, especially in cases where the major parties have left their voters to fend for themselves in a globalized economy.

This crisis may continue for as long as four years. Public life may be impaired and civility permanently weakened. Grandiosity and an increase in risk-taking behavior may lead to a rise in the racial temperature and the loss of old friendships. It is not yet clear if the Trump Effect can be remedied by treatment with tariffs, subsidies, and border defenses involving moats and alligators—or if these are actually signs of its terminal phase. It may in fact be incurable, like senility and other symptoms of decay.

Worse, the Trump Effect can jump like a virus from one sick constitution to another. Named for its first appearance in the United States in early November 2016, within weeks the Trump Effect claimed its first European victim. The Italian prime minister was overthrown in a referendum on constitutional reform. In their presidential election, 46 percent of Austrians showed symptoms, voting for Norbert Hofer and the anti-immigrant Freedom party. A full-scale epidemic is expected in 2017, with significant outbreaks of populism in France, Italy, Germany, Holland, and Britain. Further complications may induce the amputation of the southern tier of the European Union.

Pundits have correctly diagnosed one thing: the symptoms of America's domestic problems and the possible effects of a Trump presidency on America's global position. But their assumption that Trump's victory makes electoral revolts in Europe more likely is erroneous. Europe's insurrections may arise for similar reasons, and may even take similar form, but correlation, as the analysts hate to admit, is not causality. Europeans and Americans may face similar challenges in a globalized economy, but they are heirs to different histories.

Biblical Jihad

Trump appointed a white nationalist, Steve Bannon, as chief White House strategist — which was promptly celebrated by the American Nazi Party and the Ku Klux Klan. The incoming vice president, Mike Pence, has not elicited the same reaction, instead often painted as the reasonable adult on the ticket, a "counterbalance" to Trump and a "bridge to the establishment." However, there is every reason to regard him as, if anything, even more terrifying than the president-elect.

Mike Pence was raised Catholic, in a Kennedy Democrat household, but he has been a devout evangelical since being converted at a Christian music festival in Kentucky while in college. Pence now describes himself as "a Christian, a Conservative, and a Republican, in that order." Even his political action committee's name gives off a crusader vibe: Principles Exalt a Nation.

Pence's ascent to the second most powerful position in the U.S. government is a tremendous coup for the radical religious right. Pence — and his fellow Christian supremacist militants — would not have been able to win the White House on their own. For them, Donald Trump was a godsend. *"This may not be our preferred candidate, but that doesn't mean it may not be God's candidate to do something that we don't see,"* said David Barton, a prominent Christian-right activist and president of Wall Builders, an organization dedicated to making the U.S. government enforce "biblical values." In June, Barton prophesied: *"We may look back in a few years and say, 'Wow, [Trump] really did some things that none of us expected.'"*

Trump is a Trojan horse for a cabal of vicious zealots who have long craved an extremist Christian theocracy, and Pence is one of its most prized warriors. With Republican control of the House and Senate and the prospect of dramatically and decisively tilting the balance of the Supreme Court to the far right, the incoming administration will have a real shot at bringing the fire and brimstone of the second coming to Washington.

"The enemy, to them, is secularism. They want a God-led government. That's the only legitimate government," contends Jeff Sharlet, author of two books on the radical religious right, including "The Family: The Secret Fundamentalism at the Heart of American Power." *"So when they speak of business, they're speaking not of something separate from God, but they're speaking of what, in*

Mike Pence's circles, would be called biblical capitalism, the idea that this economic system is God-ordained."

While Trump has flip-flopped on a variety of issues, from abortion to immigration to war and health care, Pence has been a reliable stalwart throughout his public life in the cause of Christian jihad — never wavering in his commitment to America-First militarism, the criminalizing of abortion, and utter hatred for gay people (*unless they go into conversion therapy "to change their sexual behavior," which Pence has suggested the government pay for*).

He supported making the Patriot Act permanent and wants to ban the burning of the U.S. flag. Pence does not believe federal law enforcement agencies should have to get a FISA warrant to conduct domestic surveillance and voted against requiring any warrant for domestic wiretapping. As governor of Indiana, he did quietly sign a bill to limit the use of Stingray devices by local law enforcement, though it was during the early stages of the Snowden revelations and the public concern about government surveillance was intense.

Pence supported giving retroactive immunity to telecom companies implicated in warrantless surveillance. He does not want congressional oversight of CIA interrogations — which Trump believes should include waterboarding and other torture "a hell of a lot worse than waterboarding." Pence has paid lip service to the illegality of torture but said that "enhanced interrogation" has saved lives. He has characterized relationship-building, non-coercive interrogation strategies as "Oprah Winfrey methods." Pence is against whistleblower protections that would prohibit retaliation for reporting crimes or misdeeds. In 2002, the ACLU gave him a 7 percent rating on civil rights.

He wants the U.S. to resume the practice of holding new prisoners at Guantánamo Bay or, as Trump put it, they plan "to fill it up." Pence also supports expanded use of the military tribunal system. Pence has claimed that he wants to "economically isolate" Iran rather than engage in a military attack. But should Israel decide to conduct pre-emptive strikes against Iran's nuclear facilities, he said in 2010, *"if the world knows nothing else, let the world know this: that America will stand with Israel."*

He supported a failed legislative effort to make it U.S. policy *"to use all means necessary to confront and eliminate nuclear threats posed by the Islamic Republic of Iran, including the use of military force."* Both in rhetoric and policy, Pence has compared "radical Islam" to the "evil empire of the Soviet Union" and said that he and Trump will "name the enemy" and "marshal the resources of our nation and our allies to hunt them down and destroy them before they threaten us."

Pence supports the "wall" Trump has said he will build, believes in self-deportation, and has staked out one of the most virulent positions against the U.S. taking in refugees from Syria. In defending a proposed ban on Syrian refugees entering Indiana, Pence said it was necessary to "ensure the safety and security of all Hoosiers." He has advocated for greater militarization of the so-called war on drugs, including escalated military patrols. Pence denounced activists and others protesting recent police killings of unarmed African-Americans, charging they "seize upon tragedy in the wake of police action shootings." He said he found it offensive to "use a broad brush to accuse law enforcement of implicit bias or institutional racism and that really has got to stop." He has said that "police officers are the best of us."

Break the Deal

The election of Donald Trump signals bad news for the Iran nuclear deal, Barack Obama's signature foreign policy initiative. Calling it "*the worst deal ever negotiated,*" Trump has threatened to tear up the Joint Comprehensive Plan of Action on day one of his presidency. Supporters of the agreement and Obama allies warn that shredding the deal will only benefit Iranian hardliners, the very people it was supposed to restrain. "*The big winner in the aftermath of a Trump victory is Iran's Supreme Leader. Ali Khamenei will be able to walk away from Iran's obligations under the JCPOA while pinning the responsibility on Washington*", Suzanne Maloney - an Iran expert at the Brookings Institution – told Reuters.

Trump has offered the national security adviser position to Lt. Gen. Michael Flynn, who is well known for his anti-Muslim worldview, having called Islam a "cancer" and saying "fear of Muslims is rational." The position of national security adviser does not require Senate confirmation. Flynn served as the director of the Defense Intelligence Agency under President Obama, during which time some of his subordinates invented the term "Flynn facts" to refer to the false claims Flynn frequently made, including claiming Sharia law was spreading in the United States.

Kansas Congress member Mike Pompeo, who opposed closing Guantánamo Bay prison, has been named as CIA director. In 2013, he visited the notorious U.S. prison and said of the prisoners who were on hunger strike, quote, "*It looked to me like a lot of them had put on weight.*" He's also a vocal opponent of the Iran nuclear deal.

Trump's speech at AIPAC

But I didn't come here tonight to pander to you about Israel. That's what politicians do: all talk, no action. Believe me. I came here to speak to you about where I stand on the future of American relations with our strategic ally, our unbreakable friendship and our cultural brother, the only democracy in the Middle East, the state of Israel.

My number-one priority is to dismantle the disastrous deal with Iran. I have been in business a long time. I know deal-making. And let me tell you, this deal is catastrophic for America, for Israel and for the whole of the Middle East.

The problem here is fundamental. We've rewarded the world's leading state sponsor of terror with $150 billion, and we received absolutely nothing in return. I've studied this issue in great detail, I would say actually greater by far than anybody else. Believe me. Oh, believe me. And it's a bad deal.

The biggest concern with the deal is not necessarily that Iran is going to violate it because already, you know, as you know, it has, the bigger problem is that they can keep the terms and still get the bomb by simply running out the clock. And of course, they'll keep the billions and billions of dollars that we so stupidly and foolishly gave them. The deal doesn't even require Iran to dismantle its military nuclear capability. Yes, it places limits on its military nuclear program for only a certain number of years, but when those restrictions expire, Iran will have an industrial-sized, military nuclear capability ready to go and with zero provision for delay, no matter how bad Iran's behavior is. Terrible, terrible situation that we are all placed in and especially Israel.

When I'm president, I will adopt a strategy that focuses on three things when it comes to Iran. First, we will stand up to Iran's aggressive push to destabilize and dominate the region.

Iran is a very big problem and will continue to be. But if I'm not elected president, I know how to deal with trouble. And believe me, that's why I'm going to be elected president, folks. And we are leading in every poll. Remember that, please.

Iran is a problem in Iraq, a problem in Syria, a problem in Lebanon, a problem in Yemen and will be a very, very major problem for Saudi Arabia. Literally every day, Iran provides more and better weapons to support their puppet states. Hezbollah, Lebanon received — and I'll tell you what, it has received sophisticated anti-ship weapons, anti-aircraft weapons and GPS systems and rockets like very few people anywhere in the world and certainly very few countries have. Now they're in Syria trying to establish another front against Israel from the Syrian side of the Golan Heights.

In Gaza, Iran is supporting Hamas and Islamic jihad. And in the West Bank, they're openly offering Palestinians $7,000 per terror attack and $30,000 for every Palestinian terrorist's home that's been destroyed. A deplorable, deplorable situation. Iran is financing military forces throughout the Middle

East and it's absolutely incredible that we handed them over $150 billion to do even more toward the many horrible acts of terror.

Secondly, we will totally dismantle Iran's global terror network which is big and powerful, but not powerful like us. Iran has seeded terror groups all over the world. During the last five years, Iran has perpetuated terror attacks in 25 different countries on five continents. They've got terror cells everywhere, including in the Western Hemisphere, very close to home. Iran is the biggest sponsor of terrorism around the world. And we will work to dismantle that reach, believe me, believe me.

Third, at the very least, we must enforce the terms of the previous deal to hold Iran totally accountable. And we will enforce it like you've never seen a contract enforced before, folks, believe me.

Iran has already, since the deal is in place, test-fired ballistic missiles three times. Those ballistic missiles, with a range of 1,250 miles, were designed to intimidate not only Israel, which is only 600 miles away, but also intended to frighten Europe and someday maybe hit even the United States. And we're not going to let that happen. We're not letting it happen. And we're not letting it happen to Israel, believe me.

Do you want to hear something really shocking? As many of the great people in this room know, painted on those missiles in both Hebrew and Farsi were the words "Israel must be wiped off the face of the earth." You can forget that.

What kind of demented minds write that in Hebrew? And here's another. You talk about twisted. Here's another twisted part. Testing these missiles does not even violate the horrible deal that we've made. The deal is silent on test missiles. But those tests do violate the United Nations Security Council resolutions. The problem is no one has done anything about it. We will, we will. I promise, we will.

Which brings me to my next point, the utter weakness and incompetence of the United Nations. The United Nations is not a friend of democracy, it's not a friend to freedom, it's not a friend even to the United States of America where, as you know, it has its home. And it surely is not a friend to Israel.

When I'm president, believe me, I will veto any attempt by the UN to impose its will on the Jewish state. It will be vetoed 100 percent.

You see, I know about deal-making. That's what I do. I wrote "The Art of the Deal." One of the best-selling, all-time — and I mean, seriously, I'm saying one of because I'll be criticized when I say "the" so I'm going to be very diplomatic — one of... I'll be criticized. I think it is number one, but why take a chance?

One of the all-time best-selling books about deals and deal- making. To make a great deal, you need two willing participants. We know Israel is willing to deal. Israel has been trying.

That's right. Israel has been trying to sit down at the negotiating table without preconditions for years. You had Camp David in 2000 where Prime Minister Barak made an incredible offer, maybe even too generous; Arafat rejected it.

In 2008, Prime Minister Olmert made an equally generous offer. The Palestinian Authority rejected it also. Then John Kerry tried to come up with a framework and Abbas didn't even respond, not even to the secretary of state of the United States of America. They didn't even respond.

When I become president, the days of treating Israel like a second-class citizen will end on day one. And when I say something, I mean it, I mean it.

I will meet with Prime Minister Netanyahu immediately. I have known him for many years and we'll be able to work closely together to help bring stability and peace to Israel and to the entire region. Meanwhile, every single day you have rampant incitement and children being taught to hate Israel and to hate the Jews. It has to stop.

When you live in a society where the firefighters are the heroes, little kids want to be firefighters. When you live in a society where athletes and movie stars are the heroes, little kids want to be athletes and movie stars. In Palestinian society, the heroes are those who murder Jews. We can't let this continue. We can't let this happen any longer.

You cannot achieve peace if terrorists are treated as martyrs. Glorifying terrorists is a tremendous barrier to peace. It is a horrible, horrible way to think. It's a barrier that can't be broken. That will end and it'll end soon, believe me.

In Palestinian textbooks and mosques, you've got a culture of hatred that has been fomenting there for years. And if we want to achieve peace, they've got to go out and they've got to start this educational process. They have to end education of hatred. They have to end it and now.

There is no moral equivalency. Israel does not name public squares after terrorists. Israel does not pay its children to stab random Palestinians. You see, what President Obama gets wrong about deal-making is that he constantly applies pressure to our friends and rewards our enemies.

And you see that happening all the time, that pattern practiced by the president and his administration, including former Secretary of State Hillary Clinton, who is a total disaster, by the way.

She and President Obama have treated Israel very, very badly. But it's repeated itself over and over again and has done nothing (to) embolden those who hate America. We saw that with releasing the $150 billion to Iran in the hope that they would magically join the world community. It didn't happen.

President Obama thinks that applying pressure to Israel will force the issue. But it's precisely the opposite that happens. Already half of the population of Palestine has been taken over by the Palestinian ISIS and Hamas, and the other half refuses to confront the first half, so it's a very difficult situation that's never going to get solved unless you have great leadership right here in the United States.

We'll get it solved. One way or the other, we will get it solved. But when the United States stands with Israel, the chances of peace really rise and rises exponentially. That's what will happen when Donald Trump is president of the United States.

We will move the American embassy to the eternal capital of the Jewish people, Jerusalem. And we will send a clear signal that there is no daylight between America and our most reliable ally, the state of Israel.

The Palestinians must come to the table knowing that the bond between the United States and Israel is absolutely, totally unbreakable. They must come to the table willing and able to stop the terror being committed on a daily basis against Israel. They must do that.

And they must come to the table willing to accept that Israel is a Jewish state and it will forever exist as a Jewish state. I love the people in this room. I love

Israel. I love Israel. I've been with Israel so long in terms of I've received some of my greatest honors from Israel, my father before me, incredible. My daughter, Ivanka, is about to have a beautiful Jewish baby.

The Jewish Lobby

First, of the 28 Jewish members of Congress, 19 effectively voted in favor of the JCPOA, while nine opposed, including the one Jewish Republican (Lee Zeldin) in the House. Of the Democratic opponents, seven Jewish senators supported the deal. Only two Jewish senators—Chuck Schumer and Ben Cardin—opposed it. In the House, 11 Democratic members voted to approve it; nine were opposed.

This is important for no other reason than to clarify once and for all that there is no Jewish monolith that automatically supports Israeli government policies come what may. And although Democratic support among Jewish members of Congress for the JCPOA may be partially explained by party loyalty and not wishing to undermine a Democratic president, it appears from their various statements that this was not an easy decision.

Moreover, polls of Jewish opinion about the deal also showed serious divisions within the Jewish community. One survey, sponsored by the Los Angeles Jewish Journal and conducted by Social Science Research Solutions in mid-July, interviewed 501 Jews across the country. It asked respondents for their views on "an agreement reached in which the United States and other countries would lift major economic sanctions against Iran, in exchange for Iran restricting its nuclear program in a way that makes it harder for it to produce nuclear weapons." Almost half (49%) of Jewish respondents said they supported such a deal, while 31% opposed. That was a substantially higher approval rate than when the same question was asked to a representative sample of the national population (28% support, 24% oppose; 48% "don't know enough to say"). Asked whether Congress should vote to approve or oppose the deal, 53% of Jews opted for approval against 35% for opposition.

A second poll of 1,030 U.S. Jews, was conducted from Aug 7 to 22 as part of the latest annual survey of Jewish public opinion undertaken by the American Jewish Committee (AJC). Its question about the JCPOA was much less detailed: "Recently, the U.S. along with five other countries, reached a deal on Iran's nuclear program. Do you approve or disapprove of this agreement?" It's relevant to note that the AJC officially opposed approval of the JCPOA.

The result: a slight majority (50.6%) approved (16.4% percent "strongly," 34.2% "somewhat"). Just over 47% said they opposed the agreement. When asked a similar question—"Do you support or oppose the nuclear deal with Iran?"—in a national Quinnipiac University poll conducted August 20-25, respondents were far less supportive: 25% said they support the "nuclear deal" and 55% opposed it. Anti-deal organizations such as CFNI and The Israel Project aggressively touted this result.

Yet another survey of the general public conducted August 17-20 by the University of Maryland found that the more information respondents were given about the deal and its pros and cons, the more likely they were to support it. After assessing detailed arguments for and against the JCPOA, as well as alternatives proposed by critics of the deal, a 55% percent majority concluded that Congress should approve it, while 44% said it should be rejected. Indeed, polls that described the deal in terms of a trade-off in which sanctions against Iran would be eased in exchange for limiting its nuclear program have consistently shown much more support for congressional approval than those surveys such as AJC's and Quinnipiac's that failed to describe the details of the agreement.

The AJC survey deserves attention for other reasons relating to Iran. Respondents were asked to choose three out of 10 issues that they considered were likely to be most important in determining how they would vote in the 2016 presidential election. Only 3.8% chose "Iran's nuclear program" as their top priority, while a little over six percent of respondents cited it as their second and third choices. The economy, health care, immigration, income equality, national security, Supreme Court appointments, and U.S.-Israel relations were all given higher priority.

Asked to identify "the biggest threat to the United States today" from a list that included China, Iran, ISIS, North Korea, Russia, and none of the above, Iran, at 9.5%, ranked behind ISIS (51%), China (12.8%), and Russia (10.1%).

For a longer, rather tendentious analysis (note the lead paragraph) of how AJC's respondents reacted to the Iran deal itself, the following is taken from the organization's press release about the survey:

U.S. Jews offer conflicting, and seemingly contradictory, views on the agreement reached between the P5+1 and Iran on July 14. A clear majority of American Jews lack confidence in the deal. Only 5 percent are "very confident,"

31 percent "somewhat confident," 30 percent "not so confident," and 33 percent "not confident at all" that the deal will prevent Iran from developing nuclear weapons.

While 51 percent of total respondents approve of the deal and 47 percent disapprove, there is a significant split within the community on the issue: those who consider being Jewish very important, those who view caring about Israel as a key part of their Jewish identity, and those belonging to the traditional denominations of Judaism are far more likely to oppose the deal than others. It may, in fact, be appropriate, in light of the data, to speak of two diverging Jewish sub-communities.

Among those who consider their being Jewish "very" important, 61 percent disapprove of the agreement (37 percent "strongly"), while 38 percent approve it (12 percent "strongly"). In contrast, 55 percent of those for whom being Jewish is "fairly" important approve the deal (15 percent "strongly"), as do 59 percent of those for whom being Jewish is not important (22 percent "strongly").

Similarly, a majority—54 percent—of those for whom caring about Israel is an important component of their Jewish identity disapprove of the deal, 19 percent "strongly," while 66 percent of those for whom caring about Israel is not an important component agree with the deal, 27 percent "strongly."

Fully 67 percent of Orthodox and Conservative Jews disapprove of the agreement, 45 percent "strongly." Yet 54 percent of Reform and Reconstructionist Jews approve of it (19 percent "strongly"), as do 69 percent of those who identify as "just Jewish" (24 percent "strongly").

The survey also found a fairly widespread lack of confidence in the ability of the U.S. and the International Atomic Energy Agency (IAEA), the UN body tasked with overseeing implementation of the Iran agreement, to monitor Tehran's compliance. Only 6 percent are "very confident," while 38 percent are "somewhat confident," 28 percent "not so confident," and 26 percent "not at all confident."

The survey data suggest that the best predictor, of all the variables, for attitudes towards the agreement is political party affiliation. Jewish self-described Democrats, who comprised 49 percent of those surveyed, are far more likely to support it, and Republicans, who comprised 19 percent of those surveyed, are far more likely to oppose it. According to the survey, 66 percent of Democrats approve of the agreement (22 percent "approve strongly" and 44 percent "approve somewhat"), while 87 percent of Republicans disapprove of the agreement (20 percent "disapprove somewhat" and 67 percent "disapprove strongly").

Attitudes towards the deal also vary by age. Among respondents 18- to 29-years-old, 58 percent approve, and 38 percent disapprove of the deal. For the 30- to 44-years-old cohort, 53 percent approve, and 44 percent disapprove of the agreement. For those 45- to 50-years-old, 48 percent approve, and 49 percent disapprove. And among the 60-and-over group, 48 percent approve and 51 percent disapprove.

Younger Jews are more confident that the deal will block Iran from getting nuclear weapons: 45 percent of those aged 18 to 29; 41 percent of those aged 30 to 44; 30 percent of those aged 45 to 59; and 33 percent of those 60 and over are confident that the agreement will prevent Iran from developing nuclear weapons.

The survey revealed that a minority of American Jews, 18 percent, believe Israel's security will be "less threatened" by the deal, while 43 percent assert that it will be "more threatened," and 38 percent say it will "stay the same."

Trump's Warriors

Bomb Iran

Amid much alarmist talk about an Iranian nuclear weapon being just around the corner, the "military option" was repeatedly and seriously discussed as the principal alternative to negotiations. In other words, people were talking about starting a war with Iran—although that is not how the option was commonly phrased.

A military attack, intended to damage the mere potential for producing weapons that others, including the attacker, already have would have been a naked and illegal act of aggression. It also would have been counterproductive in probably stimulating a decision by Iran to make a nuclear weapon that it had not previously decided to make. But that is how the alternatives were nevertheless discussed. Some who talked up the alternative of a military attack may have regarded it as more of a bluff, but for others war was an actual objective.

So in addition to the other setbacks to U.S. interests that would ensue from the United States reneging on the agreement, a U.S.-Iranian war is a potential, and highly costly, additional possible consequence. The looming danger of such a war is not, however, only a function of how the nuclear agreement is handled. The danger looms because appointments that Donald Trump is making to senior national security positions are installing at high levels of the new administration a predisposition to stoke permanent conflict with Iran, a predisposition that is far more visceral than analytical and that embodies the kind of fervor and hatred that has the risk of leading to armed conflict.

9/11 made possible the change in the American public mood necessary to sell the Iraq War. It won't, however, take anything on the scale of 9/11 (which, remember, had nothing to do with Iraq anyway) to help catalyze a war against Iran. A lesser terrorist attack, or maybe an incident at sea, could serve the purpose. Assertive, forward U.S. military operations would increase the chance of such an incident, and once an incident occurs, it can be exploited and slanted for war-making purposes beyond the facts of the incident itself.

Trump has more appointments to make relevant to policy on Iran. One can hope for appointees who will exhibit more analysis than ardor and will favor facts over fakery. But the trend so far is not promising. Some persons mentioned for important sub-cabinet posts have been dedicated to killing the nuclear accord.

The Iraq War came about partly because enough people who had been committed to that expedition for years were put in positions of power to get an inexperienced president—for whom the war served other role-defining purposes—to go along. Now we are about to get the least prepared president in U.S. history, with little capacity on his part for questioning whatever assertions are voiced by the retired generals or others around him. At least George W. Bush, although lacking foreign policy experience, could have learned something from his father, who had been president, envoy to the United Nations and to China, and director of central intelligence. Donald Trump's father was, like Donald, a real estate developer.

Then there are the hard-core neo-cons, including ones who were crestfallen when it appeared that Trump's nomination marked an end to neoconservative dominance of Republican Party foreign policy. Some of these people became declared never-Trumpers and a few even hitched their wagons to Hillary Clinton's candidacy. But many of these people, upon hearing what the early appointees say about Iran, must now be licking their chops. In their view, the lesson for Iran of the U.S. invasion of Iraq (and never mind the subsequent eight-plus years of unpleasantness) has been: you're next.

A U.S. war with Iran would be disastrous for all interests except Iranian hardliners, ISIS and those who exploit Middle Eastern instability, others in the region doing ignoble things from which they would like to divert attention, and speculators who are long on the price of oil. Iran would strike back asymmetrically at times and places of its choosing, and the United States would help make enduring Iranian hostility a reality and not just a prejudicial preconception, and would do so not just among the hardliners. A messy and bloody Middle East would become messier and bloodier.

Those in the United States who correctly want to avoid such a calamity should take the early Trump appointments as a warning sign. The appointments especially ought to be a wake-up call for those who were too focused on Hillary Clinton's hawkishness, or too encouraged by Trump's utterances suggesting he would have a less interventionist foreign policy, or too inclined to dismiss both major party candidates as equally lost causes, to anticipate the current prospects regarding policy toward Iran.

Michael Flynn

The most important figure in this picture apart from the president-elect himself is his choice as national security adviser, Michael Flynn. Flynn's attitude toward Iran is a corollary of his broader Islamophobic view of the Muslim world, in that it involves perceptions that are out of right field if not downright bizarre. If his preconceived notions about such topics do not fit the facts, then he tries to make the facts conform.

One incident reported by the *New York Times* involved the attack on the U.S. diplomatic compound in Benghazi, Libya in 2012. Flynn insisted Iran had a role in the attack, and he told subordinates at the Defense Intelligence Agency, of which he was then the director, that their job was to find evidence that he was right. No evidence of any Iranian role in the attack has surfaced. We should not be surprised that someone who performed his duties as an intelligence chief in this manner has more recently shown an affinity for fake news of other sorts that fits his political objectives, such as alleged involvement by the Democratic presidential nominee in pedophilia rings.

Ingredients are falling, tragically, into place for a possible war with Iran. We have seen this play before, although some of the cast has changed. Flynn's leaning on intelligence officers to scrape together evidence to support his predetermined, and false, assertion about Iranian culpability in Benghazi eerily resembles the leaning by the George W. Bush White House, led by Vice President Cheney, on intelligence officers to scrape together evidence to support the predetermined, and false, assertion that the Iraqi regime of Saddam Hussein was allied with Al Qaeda.

Retired U.S. Army Lieutenant General Michael Flynn served as the director of the Defense Intelligence Agency (DIA) from 2012 to 2014. Previously, Flynn was a senior intelligence officer for the International Security Assistance Force (ISAF), U.S. Central Command (CENTCOM), the Joint Staff, and Joint Special Operations Command (JSOC).

A vocal supporter of Trump's 2016 presidential campaign, Flynn will likely champion more aggressive Middle East policies, particularly on Iran, from his perch at the National Security Council. He has been a vociferous opponent of the 2015 Iran nuclear deal, claiming it will lead to war, has pushed for "regime change" in Tehran, and has tweeted that "fear of Muslims is RATIONAL." Flynn has also called for withdrawing U.S. support for the Israel-Palestinian peace process, ending decades of U.S. efforts to resolve the conflict.

At a 2014 event at the Sheldon Adelson-backed Endowment for Middle East Truth, Flynn said, "*I don't think there's gonna peace between Israel and Palestine.*" He added: "*So let's be honest about this and not have another big name going in there and getting in the middle of the two countries and try to figure this out while people that are coming from one side of that line with daggers are putting knives into women and children in Israel.*"

Flynn's appointment has come under increasing scrutiny because of his penchant for spreading fake news on Twitter. A December 2016 report by Politico reported that Flynn used social media to boost at least 16 fake news items during the second half of 2016. "*Flynn, who has 106,000 Twitter followers, has used the platform to retweet accusations that Clinton is involved with child sex trafficking and has 'secretly waged war' on the Catholic Church, as well as charges that Obama is a 'jihadi' who 'laundered' money for Muslim terrorists.*"

Flynn spent more than thirty three years in Army intelligence, and as Director of the Defense Intelligence Agency worked closely with Generals Stanley McChrystal and David Petraeus, Admiral Mike Mullen, Director of National Intelligence James Clapper, and other policy, defense, intelligence, and war-fighting leaders. From coordinating on-the-ground operations in Iraq, Afghanistan, and elsewhere, to building reliable intelligence networks, to preparing strategic plans for fighting terrorism, Flynn has been a firsthand witness to government screw-ups, smokescreens, and censored information that our leaders don't want us to know.

DIA

Founded in 1961, the Defense Intelligence Agency has long been in the shadow of the Central Intelligence Agency, and with the end of the Cold War it lost its primary mission of collecting and analyzing information about the Soviet military. Strained by a decade of conflict in Afghanistan and Iraq, it was performing an uncertain role within the constellation of American spy agencies when Mr. Flynn arrived at headquarters in mid-2012.

The agency's system of human intelligence collection was perceived as largely broken. The effort to rebuild it was underway when Mr. Flynn took control in

2012, but he made it immediately known that he had a dim view of the agency's recent performance.

During a tense gathering of senior officials at an off-site retreat, he gave the assembled group a taste of his leadership philosophy, according to one person who attended the meeting and insisted on anonymity to discuss classified matters. Mr. Flynn said that the first thing everyone needed to know was that he was always right. His staff would know they were right, he said, when their views melded to his. The room fell silent, as employees processed the lecture from their new boss.

Current and former employees said Mr. Flynn had trouble adjusting his style for an organization with a 16,500-person work force that was 80 percent civilian. He was used to a strict military chain of command, and was at times uncomfortable with the often-messy give-and-take that is common among intelligence analysts.

Some also described him as a Captain Queeg-like character, paranoid that his staff members were undercutting him and credulous of conspiracy theories. At times, the general also exhibited what a number of officials described as tone-deafness on the larger strategic challenges confronting the nation.

The most glaring example came in early March 2014, just after Russia had seized Crimea. American officials were weighing whether to impose sanctions in response, but Mr. Flynn was pushing ahead with plans to travel to Moscow to build on an existing intelligence-sharing initiative with his Russian counterparts. He also wanted to invite Russian military intelligence officials to Washington to discuss the threat of Islamist militants. His superiors ordered both canceled.

By the end of his tenure, he had largely cut out senior staff members from significant decision-making, relying instead on a small circle of trusted advisers he had come to know during his overseas military deployments.

His bosses — Michael G. Vickers, the under secretary of defense for intelligence, and James R. Clapper, the director of national intelligence — came to think that the agency was adrift, and that Mr. Flynn refused to address its biggest problems.

"*Regrettably, he got engaged in an increasingly bitter and organizationally paralyzing feud with his senior staff when he should have been focused on building the intelligence capabilities*" of the agency, said Mr. Vickers, who was Mr. Flynn's immediate boss at the Pentagon.

During his tour in Iraq, he served under Gen. Stanley A. McChrystal, running intelligence for the military's Joint Special Operations Command, whose relentless campaign of raids and airstrikes hollowed out Al Qaeda in Iraq. When General McChrystal went to run the war in Afghanistan in 2009, Mr. Flynn signed on as his intelligence chief.

"*He wasn't a staid intelligence officer. He was aggressive. He was about the mission*," said Richard M. Frankel, a former senior F.B.I. official who worked with Mr. Flynn at the Office of the Director of National Intelligence. "*He can have sharp elbows because he is about the mission.*"

He burnished his reputation as an intelligence officer — but also for controversy. He co-wrote a paper, "Fixing Intel," that offered an early hint of his disdain for the civilian intelligence analysts he would later clash with at the Defense Intelligence Agency. Published by a Washington think tank, it bluntly stated that "*the U.S. intelligence community is only marginally relevant to the overall strategy,*" infuriating officials at the D.I.A. and the C.I.A.

More problematic from the military's perspective was Mr. Flynn's willingness to share intelligence with other countries. He returned to Washington at the end of 2010, and found himself under investigation for sharing sensitive data with Pakistan about the Haqqani network, arguably the most capable faction of the Taliban, and for providing highly classified intelligence to British and Australian forces fighting in Afghanistan.

His superiors eventually concluded that he was trying to prod Pakistan to crack down on the Haqqanis (they have yet to do so), and the general remains unapologetic about sharing intelligence with British and Australian forces. "*They're our closest allies! I mean, really, we're fighting together and I can't share a single piece of paper?*" he said in an interview last year.

Hatred of Islam

Flynn appears to hold particular animosity for Islam, which he calls a "*vicious cancer.*" In a video made just before his appearance at the 2016 GOP convention Flynn lashed out at the prophet Muhammad, blaming Islam for the Middle East's failure to "*become modern*". He then attacked Islam as a "*quote-unquote religion*" saying "*if they want to have their religion, their quote-unquote religion, and they want to have their security, and they want to pretend like they have women's rights, and they pretend like everything's fine ... I can tell you, it's not.*" Regarding the Quran, he said "*honestly, we're dealing with a text that is ancient and not helpful and a society that lives on that text and it can't come to grips with modernity, with becoming modern.*"

Bloomberg View columnist Eli Lake, for example, described Flynn as having "*spoken and written at length about combating radical Islam, not just the most extreme terrorist groups inspired by this ideology.*" And mainstream publications like Politico and The New York Times have published articles focusing on Flynn's fixation on combating "radical Islam," which Flynn sometimes acknowledges is separate from, although closely related to, the Islamic religion.

But a video published by Dinesh D'Souza's "head researcher," Kimberly Dvorak, shows Flynn engaging in a lengthy interview one day before his speech at the GOP convention in Cleveland:

"*I always say use the phrase "invest in civility and not in conflict." If you invest in civility you're helping a nation, you are challenging a nation. So, like Kuwait or the UAE or the Saudis or Egypt or any one of them. You're challenging them to take a hard look at their entire system, their entire ecosystem, because if they want to have their religion, their quote-unquote religion, and they want to have their security, and they want to pretend like they have women's rights, and they pretend like everything's fine, ... I can tell you, it's not.*

In 2015, there were more books translated in Spain, that year, in one year, translated into Spanish, than there were books translated in the Arab world for the last thousand years. OK? So a thousand years ago, the Arab world would have had all the Nobel prizes – Science, Art, Peace – they would have them all a thousand years ago, so what changed was this guy Muhammad comes into play and, honestly, we're dealing with a text that is ancient and not helpful and a society that lives on that text and it can't come to grips with modernity, with becoming modern."

Flynn regularly calls for a "reformation" of Islam, praising Egyptian President Abdel Fattah el-Sisi for cracking down on the Muslim Brotherhood. But his remarks in the video go considerably further, saying that Islam's central figure and core tenets are the impediment to progress in the Middle East.

Flynn's remarks are particularly troubling, given that the 1.6 billion Muslims who constitute approximately 23% of the world's population are members of a religion he holds incompatible with modernity.

Ledeen's influence

Around the same time, he was also getting to know Michael A. Ledeen, a controversial writer and former Reagan administration official. The two men connected immediately, sharing a similar worldview and a belief that America was in a world war against Islamist militants allied with Russia, Cuba and North Korea. That worldview is what Mr. Flynn came to be best known for during the presidential campaign, when he argued that the United States faced a singular, overarching threat, and that there was just one accurate way to describe it: "radical Islamic terrorism."

Ledeen a fear-mongering book about an alleged alliance between Islamic jihadists and former Cold War foes who are "united in their hatred of the democratic West." The book, called *The Field of Fight: How We Can Win the Global War against Radical Islam and Its Allies,* argues that the United States must engage in a multi-generational war against this "formidable" alliance, which may require sending in troops to fight battles across the globe and harnessing all available resources *"similar to the effort during World War II or the Cold War."*

The Field of Fight succinctly lays out why we have failed to stop terrorist groups from growing, and what we must do to stop them. The core message is that if you understand your enemies, it's a lot easier to defeat them—but because our government has concealed the actions of terrorists like Osama bin Laden and groups like ISIS and al Qaeda, and the role of Iran in the rise of radical Islam, we don't fully understand the enormity of the threat they pose against us.

Flynn and Ledeen write: *"If, as PC apologists tell us, there is no objective basis for members of one culture to criticize another, then it is very hard to see … the existence of an international alliance of evil countries and movements that is working to destroy us. Yet, the alliance exists, and we've already dithered for many years. The war is on. We face a working coalition that extends from North Korea and China to Russia, Iran, Syria, Cuba, Bolivia, Venezuela, and Nicaragua.*

We are under attack, not only from nation-states directly, but also from al Qaeda, Hezbollah, ISIS, and countless other terrorist groups. Suffice to say, the same sort of cooperation binds together jihadis, Communists, and garden-variety tyrants."

Sharia is the basic legal system derived from the religious precepts of Islam, mainly the Koran and the hadiths (supposedly verbatim quotes of what the prophet Muhammad said during his life). In its strictest definition, Sharia, is considered the infallible law of God. They want to impose a worldwide system based on their version of Sharia law that denies freedoms of conscience, choices, and liberties. Basic freedoms! [...] I firmly believe that Radical Islam is a tribal cult and must be crushed. Critics get buried in the details of the sunna, hadiths, the umma and the musings of countless Muslim clerics and imams. These so-called Islamic scholars keep their message so complicated so as to create chaos, to confuse in order to control. Now, Pol Pot, Stalin, and Mussolini were transparent. Sharia is a violent law that is buried in barbaric conviction.

Perhaps the scariest part about this to a man who grew up in tiny Rhode Island is that the Organization of Islamic Cooperation (OIC) now says if we criticize the Prophet or Islam, we can be charged with blasphemy. That is like saying as a Roman Catholic (and a Saint Mary's School-educated Catholic at that), I cannot criticize the priest who raped and the cardinals and bishops who cover it up!

Muslims want to apply Sharia law by using our own legal system to strengthen what many Americans believe to be a violent religious law that has no place in the United States

Putin

Despite his claims about Russia in the book he coauthored with Ledeen, Flynn has appeared to develop close relations with Russia's Vladimir Putin, raising concerns among both Democrats and Republicans. In 2015, he gave a paid speech at a Kremlim-controlled RT television network party, after which he sat next to Putin during dinner. When questioned whether the "optics" of the event could be problematic, he said that *"he didn't have any problem"* and that he wanted to make sure "they" understand that *"we have people in our country who aren't going to apologize for who they are."* He then added that one of the things *"he learned"* at the event was that *"Putin has no respect for the United States leadership. Not for the United States, but the leadership."*

On Iran

Flynn has also stated that U.S. "unwillingness to fight" creates more danger for the United States than the "arrogance of American power." He told the Daily Beast in January 2015: "The dangers to the U.S. do not arise from the arrogance of American power, but from unpreparedness or an excessive unwillingness to fight when fighting is necessary."

Flynn has long sought to push a more aggressive approach on Iran. Days after Islamist militants stormed the American diplomatic compound in Benghazi, Libya, in 2012, Lt. Gen. Michael T. Flynn reached a conclusion that stunned some of his subordinates at the Defense Intelligence Agency: Iran had a role in the attack, he told them.

For instance, according to the New York Times, Flynn sought to use the 2012 attack on the U.S. compound in Benghazi as a ploy against Iran. Soon after the Benghazi incident, he *took to pushing analysts to find Iran's hidden hand in the disaster*", according to current and former officials familiar with the episode. But like many other investigations into Benghazi, theirs found no evidence of any links, and the general's stubborn insistence reminded some officials at the agency of how the Bush administration had once relentlessly sought to connect Saddam Hussein and Iraq to the Sept. 11, 2001, attacks.

In a March 2015 interview with Fox News Flynn declared that the Obama administration intentionally remains ignorant about issues in the Middle East. He argued that the United States is working with "almost a policy of willful ignorance," adding that "we are talking to Iran about a nuclear deal with this almost complete order of breakdown in the Middle East."

Flynn was critical of the Obama administration's diplomatic efforts to resolve the Iranian nuclear dispute and denounced the July 2015 nuclear agreement reached between Iran and the P5+1 world powers. He has stated that the United States gets "nothing but grief" from the deal and has outlandishly proclaimed that it will lead to *"the elimination of Israel"* and a *"large regional war."*

Flynn is an advisor to the anti-Iran deal group Veterans Against the Deal, which partnered with the American Security Initiative (AIC) to run TV ads opposing the deal in the run up to Congress's September 17, 2015 deadline to vote on the agreement. AIC's board includes avowedly militarist figures like former Sens. Norm Coleman (R-MN) and Joe Lieberman (I-CT).

In June 2015, Flynn testified on Iran before the U.S. House of Representatives, where he argued that "regime change" in Iran was the "best way to stop the Iranian nuclear weapons program."

Flynn's Testimony

Chairman Ros---Lehtinen and Ranking Member Deutch, members of the Joint Committee, thank you for the opportunity to present my views on Iran's missile capabilities and how they impact regional as well as global issues now and in the future, These will directly and negatively impact U.S. National Security unless we develop a long term, 100 year strategy for our Nation—there is no way around it.

Our closed, 20th Century bureaucratic system appears unable to adapt to the rapid and complex changes and threats we face in the 21st Century, especially those occurring throughout the Middle East and the wider trans---region, including Iran and Central Asia to the East, large parts of North and East Africa to the West, and many parts of Europe to the North.

These problems are exacerbated from an ever---expanding influence by the following;

The negative behavior and expanding influence of the Islamic Republic of Iran. The increasing complexity in Iraq and Syria—with absolutely no end in sight, no clear U.S. policy, nor do we have sufficient U.S. Whole of Government actions being taken by the United States

The new Middle East struggling to be born, and, if we are not careful, the United States will be left out of the growth of this region and our security at home will be placed at further risk (as the revelation of the Khorosan Group makes clear, this process is already well underway).

The unfinished revolutions in the Middle East in places such as Yemen and parts of Africa and our ongoing transition in Afghanistan are all being taken advantage of by Iran, ISIS and AQ.

The resurgence of Russian and Chinese influence in the region, especially in the energy acquisition and development arenas, weapons proliferation, and economic dominance and interdependence, all clearly impacting the security of the United States.

Not only do these impact our security at home, but they also impact our allies and friends in the region, most important, the State of Israel—Israel lives under the threat of total annihilation from Iran and other Islamic radical elements in the region—something the United States must never allow, nor should we deal equally with those who spew this type of hatred and bigotry (we would not stand for it here in this country and we should not stand for it elsewhere in the world where our closest friends are at risk).

Specifically focusing on the expanding Iranian missile development program, and failing to acknowledge the frequent warnings from our intelligence community, especially defense intelligence, regarding the hegemonic behaviors of the Islamic Republic of Iran, Iran's missile program is growing far stronger.

Both our military and our policy---making civilian elite appear to be living in closed systems. Because Second Generation war reduces everything to putting firepower on targets, when we fail against Fourth Generation opponents, our nation's leaders' (political and military) only answer is to put more firepower on more targets.

Ideas about other ways of waging war are ignored because they do not fit the closed Second Generation paradigm. Meanwhile, Washington cannot consider alternatives to our current foreign policy or grand strategy because anyone who proposes one is immediately exiled from the establishment.

Before I address a few solutions about their missile program, I want to make a short statement of things I know, things I believe, and things I don't know but suspect.

To begin, the nuclear deal, that will likely be concluded this summer, suffers from severe deficiencies.

Iran has every intention to build a nuclear weapon. They have stated it many times, they have attempted well over a decade to move rapidly to nuclearizing its capability, and their enrichment to twenty percent and their rapid move to develop a ballistic missile program, are examples of their continued preparedness to weaponize a missile for nuclear delivery.

Iran's stated desire to destroy Israel is very real. Iran has not once (not once) contributed to the greater good of the security of the region. Nor has Iran contributed to the protection of security for the people of the region. Instead, and for decades, they have contributed to the severe insecurity and instability of the region, especially the sub---region of the Levant surrounding Israel (i.e, Southern Lebanon, Gaza, and the Border region along the Golan Heights on the Syrian side of the border).

Iran killed or maimed thousands of Americans and Iraqis during our fight in Iraq during the period of 2003 to 2011, and since 2005, they have also provided limited support to the Taleban and the Gholam Yahya Front in Herat. Although the International Coalition of Nations in Iraq defeated AQ in Iraq, and despite Iranian support to AQ and Shia militias' attempts to disrupt our joint efforts to win the fight in Iraq—this has all now been squandered.

There is also the matter of incomplete verification. Iran's leaders made it clear the furthest they will go is to allow International inspectors (IAEA) only "managed access" to nuclear facilities, and only with significant prior notification. This makes it nearly impossible, as a matter of full transparency, to have real "eyes on" the state of Iranian nuclear development to include their missile program.

The notion of "snap back" sanctions is fiction. The Iranian regime is already more economically stable than it was in November of 2013, while the international sanctions coalition that brought Tehran to the table in the first place is showing serious signs of strain. It's unreasonable to believe that under these conditions we will be able to put the "Regime Sanctions Team" back together again.

Iranian rogue state behavior is on the rise and increasing. Parallel to its nuclear dialogue with the west, the Islamic Republic has stepped up its destabilizing activities in its neighborhood. This includes massive support for the Assad Regime in Syria, as well as backing for Yemen's Shi'ite Houthi rebels, covertly supporting the Taleban in Afghanistan, actively advising, assisting, and accompanying Iraqi Shia militias inside of Iraq, maintaining pressure in Lebanon, and they continue to provide weapons and other arms to Hamas in the Gaza.

From the beginning, our friends, partners and allies in the region were left out of the Joint Plan of Action (or P5+1) discussion. They simply wanted to be updated along the path of these talks and they were not (in any sort of coherent or cohesive manner). This latest attempt at a GCC summit was embarrassing for the United States. Obviously, this leaderless turnout with no serious long term, strategic agreement or framework for security coming out of the summit, you get less than acceptable results. Lesson relearned, you don't bring Arab nations together without the deal already being agreed to.

It is clear that the nuclear deal is not a permanent fix but merely a placeholder. The ten year timeframe only makes sense if the Administration truly believes that it is possible for a wider reconciliation with Iran that is likely to occur, which will make the Iranian regime change its' strategic course. That's wishful thinking.

I believe we have a major trust deficit with all the countries in the region (to include our closest partners, the Israelis).

I believe the region will continue to decline, and instability, without strong and direct US leadership and involvement respectively, will only lead to greater conflict.

I believe that Iran represents a clear and present danger to the region, and eventually to the world—they are still a U.S. State Department designated Islamic state sponsor of terrorism, they have and they continue to violate international sanctions, and they continue to spew hatred in their rhetoric coming from senior members of their government—to include their top Mullahs.

Iran's nuclear program has significant – and not fully disclosed – military dimensions. The P5+1 dialogue with Iran has glossed over a number of such programs (including warhead miniaturization blueprints) in pursuit of an agreement. However, these factors are important insofar as they signal the true aim of Iran's program. That aim will doubtless continue in the wake of any negotiated settlement that leaves the Iranian nuclear effort largely intact.

Iran's nuclear program is not a stand---alone program. The perceived acceptance of Iran's nuclear program is likely to touch off a dangerous domino effect in the region, as other countries, such as the Kingdom of Saudi Arabia, look for strategic counterweights to the emerging Iranian bomb, already manifesting in fairly open KSA outreach to Pakistan for nuclear capability.

What we don't know is the full scope of Iran's nuclear effort itself. The intelligence community does not have complete "eyes on" the totality of the Iranian nuclear program, nor can it guarantee that we have identified all of Iran's nuclear facilities and processes. Moreover, given the history of the nuclear age, it is prudent to conclude that there are elements of Iran's nuclear program that still remain hidden from view (Iran has demonstrated in their own actions, they cannot be trusted).

The true effects of Iranian nuclearization on the region are unknown and staggering. We can anticipate significant proliferation as a result of the Iranian nuclear deal, but we cannot be certain of its extent or its effects. This enormously complicates America's existing security arrangements in the Middle East, as well as the political and military guarantees we will need to provide to Iran's neighbors.

I believe that Iran's overarching strategic goals of enhancing its security, prestige, and regional influence have led it to pursue capabilities to meet its civilian goals and give it the ability to build missile---deliverable nuclear weapons, if it chooses to do so. We do not know whether Iran will eventually decide to build nuclear weapons.

I believe that Iran does not face any insurmountable technical barriers to producing a nuclear weapon, making Iran's political will the central issue. However, Iranian implementation of the Joint Plan of Action (JPOA) has at least temporarily inhibited further progress in its uranium enrichment and plutonium production capabilities and effectively eliminated Iran's stockpile of 20 percent enriched uranium. The agreement has also enhanced the transparency of Iran's nuclear activities, mainly through improved International Atomic Energy Agency (IAEA) access and earlier warning of any effort to make material for nuclear weapons using its safeguarded facilities

I believe that Tehran would choose ballistic missiles as its preferred method of delivering nuclear weapons, when it builds them. Iran's ballistic missiles are inherently capable of delivering WMD, and Tehran already has the largest inventory of ballistic missiles in the Middle East. Iran's progress on space launch vehicles—along with its desire to deter the United States and its allies—provides Tehran with the means and motivation to develop longer---range missiles, including intercontinental ballistic missiles (ICBMs).

Iran possesses a substantial inventory of theater ballistic missiles capable of reaching as far as parts of southeastern Europe. Tehran is developing increasingly sophisticated missiles and improving the range and accuracy of its other missile systems. Iran is also acquiring advanced naval and aerospace capabilities, including naval mines, small but capable submarines, coastal defense cruise missile batteries, attack craft, anti---ship missiles, and armed unmanned aerial vehicles.

As the Washington Post editorialists have said, regime change in Tehran is the best way to stop the Iranian nuclear weapons program. The same applies to their missile arsenal, which is of high quality and growing. Even today, their missiles cover most all of the Middle East, and the next generation will include ICBMs capable of attacking the American homeland.

Just look at the cooperation with North Korea, China and Russia. Connect those dot and you get the outline of a global alliance aimed at the U.S., our friends, and our allies.

Russian assistance is part of a broader pattern. After all, the Iranian nuclear reactor at Bushehr is Russian---built, the two countries work very closely together in Syria, and Russia is providing Iran with an effective antiaircraft system that could be deployed against any aircraft seeking to destroy the nuclear program.

The North Korean cooperation is also very significant, as the two countries (North Korea and Iran) have long traded expertise, not least regarding nuclear and possibly EMP weapons.

China is also deeply involved in Iran (and the rest of the region). Indeed, significant areas in the oil producing regions of Iran are under direct Chinese control, significant quantities of Iranian money are in Chinese banks, and China is a leading sanctions buster.

And finally, the U.S. intelligence community's record in tracking clandestine nuclear weapons programs has been decidedly mixed. While it has been very successful in detecting such programs, it has often failed to correctly assess their status, identify proliferation paths (especially when multiple or nontraditional paths have been taken), to locate key facilities, or track the activities of proliferation supplier networks.

For instance:

The United States had suspected for well over a decade that North Korea had a uranium enrichment program but did not learn about its centrifuge plant at Yongbyon until the plant was shown to a delegation of former U.S. officials in 2010.

The United States did not learn about the reactor that North Korea was building in Syria until it was close to completion in 2007.

The U.S. intelligence community did not become aware until nearly four years later that Iran had apparently suspended its "structured" weaponization program in 2003.

The United States did not learn about Iran's enrichment plants at Natanz and Fordow until several years after work on each had commenced—albeit several years before each became operational.

Prior to the 1991 Gulf War, the international community was unaware of the full extent and advanced status of Iraq's nuclear program, which IAEA inspectors uncovered after the war.

While South Africa had long been suspected of having a weapons program, the 1993 announcement that it had produced a half--- dozen nuclear devices was the first confirmation of this fact for the United States.

The A. Q. Khan network operated for more than a decade and assisted Libya, North Korea, Iran, and possibly others before initial steps were taken to disrupt and dismantle the network in 2001.

Moreover, a recent Defense Science Board study of nuclear monitoring and verification technologies concluded that "the technologies and processes designed for current treaty verification and inspections are inadequate to future monitoring realities" such as "identifying small or nascent [nuclear] programs."

This seems to imply that creative missile and nuclear proliferators would enjoy an advantage in the cat and mouse game they are playing with the United States and the international community.

There are a number of things that the international community can do however, to level the playing field with Iran and further reduce the chances of its violating its Nuclear Non---Proliferation treaty obligations.

Immediately direct Iran to open up all of its facilities, scientific, military, and current nuclear facilities, for international inspections.

The U.S. must take a more active role in the region for what will be a race for "nuclearization" preferring energy development over weaponization.

Provide greater authorities to all elements of U.S. National power to defeat the Islamic radicals we now call the Islamic State—put them out of business.

Immediately recognize, fully support, help organize, and assist those regional partners create an "Arab NATO---like" structure and framework. Build an Arab Army that is able to secure their regional responsibilities.

Clearly define and recognize that we face a very radicalized enemy in the likes of Islamic extremism. The administration's refusal to state what we can plainly see is beyond being irresponsible and ranges on being dangerous for the long---term security of the United States.

Seek and appoint leaders (regionally, internationally or right here at home), give them the right and appropriate authorities that can actually accomplish the strategic objectives we seek.

We should expect a far more aggressive Iran as it relates to the Gulf (both overtly and covertly) and one that will remain militarily engaged in the Levant for the foreseeable future even if Assad is overthrown. To the extent that Iranian support to the Huthis is regarded as successful we should expect to see it emulated in Bahrain and possibly eastern Saudi Arabia.

While the sectarian angle is likely to limit Iran's ability to support Sunni proxies and thereby limit their ability to project power, the ISIL crisis has created a significant cadre of Shi'a jihadists that can and will support Iran's policies through means, fair and foul.

If Iran is able to contain and defeat ISIL and subjugate, through proxies, large portions of Iraq's Sunni population, we should expect a whole host of initiatives intended to limit and eliminate Iranian influence by both state and private actors, as is now occurring in Yemen. All of this creates an environment that is rife for conflict.

Pretty much, what Prime Minister Netanyahu predicted to Congress, which was we would see the end of the Non Proliferation Treaty for all intents and purposes.

The Kingdom of Saudi Arabia, the nations of Egypt, Kuwait, the UAE, Jordan, Qatar, and Turkey will all attempt their own missile and nuclear programs with varying degrees of success and competence, and the best---case scenario is that we have our current relationship with Pakistan duplicated five fold in a region where we have seen a significant government turnover from at least 2011 to present.

And as I stated above, we, the United States of America must comprehend that evil doesn't recognize diplomacy and nations such as Iran will still maintain the intent of achieving nuclear weapon status. Despite the preaching of our current leadership—we said many of the same things in 1994 when talking to North Korea about this very same issue—and look at where North Korea is today regarding nuclear weapons proliferation.

We also have to recognize that Russia and China have demonstrated that wherever they can drive a wedge into any alliances or partnerships we have, they will. All you have to do is read the media outlets in the Middle East and see for yourself how much both are already working to get their feet fully on the ground when it comes to nuclear development in the region.

Additionally, the lack of consequences associated with Iranian behavior will also prompt other nations to develop their own proxy forces, none of which we are likely to find in keeping with US interests.

The worst---case scenario is a reversion to a pre---Yom Kippur War security environment, except with less restraint. While the sectarian angle may limit impact against Israel in the near---term, they are likely to be targeted by jihadists of either flavor (Sunni or Shia) and any Egyptian WMD efforts have to be of serious concern because the government has changed three times since 2011 and it won't be clear who is going to be on top the next time it occurs (my strongest recommendation is for the U.S. to pick President Al---Sisi as a partner and get on with assisting him fight the Islamic radicals trying to take over Egypt).

As for Israel, it sees its primary ally and patron becoming increasingly distant and a hostile power is rising against it, which may lead Israeli leadership to undertake increasing rash or desperate actions in an effort to secure immediate gains.

It's difficult to overestimate the risks manifest in an Iran armed with ballistic and / or nuclear weapons. Certainly the ambitions of those who have advocated for this capability for 30 years would be vindicated. That many of the same harbor genuine beliefs which include the responsibility of the faithful to prepare for a return of the Imamate and the end of times, often seen as concurrent with "exporting the revolution" (or the reason for being of the IRGC---QF), all of which should provide us little comfort.

The most dramatic impact would be the virtual elimination of coercion and persuasion; in nuclear deterrence there remains only warfare by proxy and Mutually Assured Destruction (MAD). Iran's possession and extended influence over a significant portion of the world's economically viable petro---chemical resources and / or the shipping lanes they require to reach markets would provide them power OPEC has never quite managed to corral.

Beyond the unbridled use of a full spectrum of surrogate forces, they would have an inordinate and immediate ability to incur deep and sustained economic costs that would alter global alliances with China as penultimate consumer, and Europe as fractured addict. The ripple effects of such control would be felt well before they were exercised, and reshape the balance of power. Confident without repercussions and satisfied behind a nuclear inventory, Iran would flex its newly acquired regional hegemony to extend the buffer well beyond its Arab neighbors and in the process neutralize internal opposition (i.e., Kurds, Ahvazis, Azeris, Baluchs) without regard to international opinion.

Sunni Arab opposition would be reflexive and likely result in an increased reliance on Russia for assistance (perhaps the real winner in the global shift in power as ally to both Iran and the only port for a listing Arab world desperately seeking military assistance). The conflict would expand, but it's worth noting that we can expect a host of pernicious and unintended consequences as Arab states fund and support any and all opposition to Iran including but not limited to, ISIS and AQ and its Associated Movements (AQAM—yes, these latter groups still exist).

While disconcerting given the expanded ranks and reach of both (exceeded only by our underestimation), the real challenge only comes into view when you consider the GCC's newest sport; acquiring WMD. North Korea, Libya, South Africa, and others had far thinner wallets and so all previous timelines and estimations are bound to be optimistic and inadequate.

Saudi Arabia has been openly planning on acquiring South Korean, French, and Japanese reactors ostensibly to power desalinization plants. Beyond their well--documented relationship with Pakistan, their options are as diverse as their portfolios. And who can question their will or their reasons?

That leaves Arabs and Persians, Sunni and Shi'a in what can only be described as a struggle of religious and deadly proportions across the spectrum of conflict and in possession of weapons, which cannot be contained, and employing surrogates who accept no boundaries (physically, virtually, geographically, or practically); all this atop half the world's oil and gas, and astride much of the world's most vital shipping lanes.

I don't see how delivery systems (missiles or sophisticated guidance) can be excluded from any "deal". Reach is as important as force, just as in boxing.

The acquisition of reliable delivery systems is as vulnerable as enrichment and weaponization and cannot be ignored. Unfortunately, it has proven profitable for all too many who feel they don't bear the consequences and I'd add testing and experimentation.

These days, it takes very unique systems to simulate, and almost certainly, simulations will proceed explosions and launches. The last thing they'd want is to telegraph failure and expose themselves to preemptive destruction.

Lastly, and I think most importantly, it's easier now to predict hurricanes, tornadoes, and earthquakes within our borders than the trajectory of the Middle East on a good day. Should ambitions be unleashed (or encouraged) while the capability to inflict damage exceeds the ambitions of the most aggressive mullah it would quite predictably result in a regional arms race—including but not limited to WMD—and open conflict for the resources to sustain it.

This would certainly shift the global balance of power, as I've described above, but the most deadly result would be entropy on a scale not seen in centuries.

We would have no way of anticipating risk, much less managing or containing it. Delusions abound these days, but anyone who can argue for an ICBM or nuclear capable Iran is more a pyromaniac than pragmatist.

Incidentally, even if we didn't believe this to be the case, our partners in the region do. Until we can reach some accord on the primacy of the Iranian threat we will never approach common ground on the secondary matters including ISIS (which they, in my judgment, view as symptomatic).

With that Chairman, again, I appreciate this invitation and you and your committee's leadership as we address our Nation's security requirements well into the future.

Drones's business

But little attention has been paid to his role as vice chairman of a small drone company, Drone Aviation Holding Corp (DAC). The corporation received a series of Department of Defense contracts after he joined the company in April, while he was simultaneously serving as an adviser to the Trump campaign. If Trump follows through on his campaign promise to deploy more surveillance drones on the Canadian and Mexican borders, DAC would be well-placed to win even bigger contracts.

The company, which is developing a line of small, tethered, surveillance aircraft, issued a statement about Flynn's new role saying that he "will work with Drone Aviation's growing list of Department of Defense ('DoD'), government agency and commercial customers to harness the unique data collection, communications and surveillance capabilities of the Company's tethered tactical aerostat and drone platforms."

Flynn's appointment to DAC's board on April 27, 2016 coincided with a series of DoD contracts that significantly contributing to the bottom line of a company valued at $25 million and whose stock currently hovers around three dollars per share.

Flynn is paid $36,000 per year for his work. He was issued 100,000 restricted shares, which will vest over two years, commencing with his appointment as a director last April. DAC also helped Flynn promote his book The Field of Fight: In March, the month before Flynn was appointed to the board, the company was awarded a DoD contract "in excess $780,000" for a lighter-than-air surveillance and communications aircraft. That contract was followed by a $194,000 "upgrade contract" for the same project.

Following Flynn formally joining the company, DAC won a $125,000 contract in August "for equipment and engineering services including the integration of an advanced sensor suite for long endurance, persistent, tethered aerial applications for a current DoD customer."

In October, they were awarded a $400,000 contract for the company's electric tethered drone and a contract "valued at more than $200,000" for communications sensors integration onto its lighter than air UAV.

Drone Aviation Holding Corp. doesn't market its products just for the DoD. Its website advertises that it "uses include border patrol, emergency response, search and rescue and law enforcement response to crowd management, hostage situations, and large event security and protection."

Trump, who took Flynn on as a campaign adviser in February, embraced the idea of utilizing UAVs for border surveillance, alongside his initial plan to build a wall across the entire 2,000-mile southern border.

Twelve days before Flynn signed his contract with DAC, Trump told Syracuse.com that, if elected president, he would expand the deployment of drones on both the Canadian and Mexican borders for 24-hour surveillance of the borders.

"They would work in conjunction with the Border Patrol, who are fantastic people who want to do their job," Trump told Syracuse.com. "I want surveillance for our borders, and the drone has great capabilities for surveillance."

According to a federal audit published in January 2015, the decade-long use of surveillance drones on the borders cost more than initially estimated and the Department of Homeland Security's inspector general found "little or no evidence" that border drones had performed effectively.

James Mattis

James "Mad Dog" Mattis is a retired U.S Marine Corps general and combat veteran who served as commander of U.S. Central Command during 2010-2013 before being removed by the Obama administration reportedly because of differences over Iran policy. Mattis has recently served on the board of directors of military contractor General Dynamics and been a visiting scholar at the conservative Hoover Institution.

Mattis is known for his penchant for making rash comments about killing people, like saying *"It's fun to shoot some people."* In a 2016 profile for the New Yorker Steve Coll wrote: *"In battle, Mattis's boldness had earned him the nickname 'Mad Dog,' and when he commanded the Marines' 1st Division during the invasion of Iraq, in 2003, his radio call sign was 'Chaos.'"*

Despite having policy differences with Trump—including over the use of torture, which Mattis seems to think is ineffective—Mattis reportedly appealed to the incoming administration because of *"his insistence that Iran is the greatest threat to peace in the Middle East, as well as his acerbic criticism of the Obama administration."*

A key Mattis booster has been Sen. John McCain (R-AZ), who pressed Trump to nominate either Mattis or retired Army Gen. Jack Keane, a colleague of several neoconservative activists. McCain's Senate colleague Sen. Kirsten Gillibrand (D-NY), however, promised to filibuster Mattis' nomination, which requires a congressional waiver because federal law requires that the head of the Pentagon be retired from the military for at least seven years. *"While I deeply respect General Mattis's service, I will oppose a waiver,"* Gillibrand said in a statement. *"Civilian control of our military is a fundamental principle of American democracy, and I will not vote for an exception to this rule."*

According to Coll, who interviewed Mattis extensively in 2011 while he was head of Central Command: "Over all, the Mattis in my notes seemed intently focused on stability, wary of warfare that sought to promote democracy or idealism, sentimental about the independence of the Baltic states, firmly committed to NATO, and unsentimental about Russia."

Some analysts have focused attention on Mattis' experience working at General Dynamics, one of the largest Pentagon contractors. For the military-industrial-congressional complex it doesn't get much better than this. Mattis was selected as an "independent director" of General Dynamics in 2013, had been paid $594,369 as of 2016, and had *"amassed more than $900,000 worth of company stock."* It reported that while on the General Dynamics board, Mattis testified before Congress, where he called caps on defense spending—known as the sequestration—a national security threat. *"No foe in the field can wreak such havoc on our security that mindless sequestration is achieving,"* he said during the 2015 hearing.

On Iran

Mattis has been an outspoken Iran hawk for many years. He has argued that the country has declared war on the United States and reportedly thinks *"that Iran's support for Shia militias in Iraq meant that Tehran was directly responsible for the deaths of hundreds of American troops."* In a little-noticed speech at the Center for Strategic and International Studies (CSIS) in April 2016, Mattis said that Iran was the *"single most enduring threat to stability and peace in the Middle East"* and *"a revolutionary cause devoted to mayhem."*

In his comments at the think tank, Mattis said that Iran posed four specific threats to the US and its allies, apart from its nuclear program: its ongoing development of advanced ballistic missiles capable of one day hitting Israel and Europe; its stated threats to block vital international waterways like the Strait of Hormuz; its increasing cyber attack capabilities; and its support for armed proxies ranging from Hezbollah in Lebanon and Syria to the Houthis who now control Yemen.

At the CSIS event he said, *"I want to make clear there's no going back. Absent a clear and present violation [by Iran], I don't think we can take advantage of some new president—Republican or Democrat—and say, 'well, we're not going to live up to our word in this agreement.' I believe we'd be alone if we did, and unilateral economic sanctions from us would not have anywhere near the impact of an allied approach to this."*

Mattis has also puzzlingly suggested that Iran may somehow be collaborating with ISIS, stating at CSIS: *"I consider ISIS nothing more than an excuse for Iran to continue its mischief [in the region]. Iran is not an enemy of ISIS; they have a lot to gain from the turmoil that ISIS creates. I would just point out one question for you to look into: What is the one country in the Middle East that has not been attacked by ISIS? One. That is Iran. That is more than happenstance, I'm sure."*

Although Mattis likely wouldn't oppose a confrontation with Iran, he hasn't openly called for one, either, and even hinted at an openness to engaging with 'Iranian generals' when he was at CENTCOM. In short, though he's an 'Iran hawk,' Mattis doesn't seem to be particularly out of the mainstream in the U.S. foreign policy community, at least not when compared to people like Flynn and Pompeo."

It is common to observe, based on congressional testimony and other public comments he has made, that Mattis has taken a hard line toward Iran, particularly the activities of the Revolutionary Guards and other allied or expeditionary Iranian militant units in Iraq, Syria, Lebanon, and Yemen. But mainly he seemed focused on deepening America's long-standing military and political alliances with Sunni Arab states—Morocco, Egypt, Jordan, Saudi Arabia, Qatar, and the United Arab Emirates. During his time at Central Command, he spent many hours talking to counterparts in those countries, which tend to view Shia revolutionary Iran as a serious threat. The smaller, militarily weaker Sunni states closest to Iran—such as the U.A.E.—were and remain acutely anxious that the United States might sell out their security in some Nixon-to-China grand bargain with Tehran.

On Iraq

Although he did not speak out publicly against the decision to invade Iraq in 2003, Mattis said at a 2015 conference that *"we will probably look back on the invasion of Iraq as a mistake—as a strategic mistake."*

At the time of the invasion, he said: *"I think people were pretty much aware that the U.S. military didn't think it was a very wise idea. But we give a cheery 'Aye aye, sir.' Because when you elect someone commander in chief—we give our advice. We generally give it in private."* Notably, Mattis did not heed this same protocol with respect to the Obama administration and Iran, *"speaking openly or critically about the Iran deal and questioning some of the Obama administration's motives,"* which ultimately led to his dismissal from Central Command.

On Israel

Despite the backing of some leading neoconservatives, Mattis has been critical of Israel and U.S. relations with the country. He has argued that Israeli settlement policy eventually leads to apartheid: *"If I'm in Jerusalem and I put 500 Jewish settlers out here to the east and there's 10,000 Arab settlers in here, if we draw the border to include them, either it ceases to be a Jewish state or you say the Arabs don't get to vote—apartheid."*

As for the negative impact of one-sided U.S. support for the country, he said in 2013: *"I paid a military security price every day as the commander of CentCom because the Americans were seen as biased in support of Israel, and that moderates all the moderate Arabs who want to be with us, because they can't come out publicly in support of people who don't show respect for the Arab Palestinians."*

Observers point out that these views are at odds with those expressed by Trump, even if real estate mogul has expressed doubts about Israel's commitment to seeking peace with the Palestinians. According to one report, the rightwing Zionist Organization of America *"issued a statement (that since appears to have been deleted from their own website) saying that Mattis's 2013 remarks 'revealed a lack of appreciation for and understanding of the extraordinary value to American security resulting from a strong American-Israeli alliance and a secure Israel"* and urging *"that Mattis not be appointed' as Defense Secretary."*

On Russia

Mattis appears to differ sharply with Trump over Russia, although the two have reportedly discussed ways to improve up relations. While Trump is a vocal admirer of Vladimir Putin, Mattis has argued that Russia's aggressive militarism is "much more severe, more serious" than both Brussels and Washington seem to think.

According to a report of a 2015 event at the ultra-conservative Heritage Foundation, Mattis warned that the "nationalist emotions that Russian President Vladimir Putin has stirred up will make it 'very, very hard [for him or his successors] to pull back from some of the statements he has made' about the West. At the same time, Putin faces problems of his own with jihadists inside Russia's borders that threaten domestic stability.

Mattis, echoing the assessments of most of the Pentagon's top brass, has a sharply different assessment of Putin, whom he sees as a clear threat to both the US and many of Washington's closest European allies.

According to an article by the US Naval Institute, Mattis used a speech to a conservative think tank last May to warn that Russia's annexation of Crimea and continued meddling in eastern Ukraine was a "severe" and "serious" threat that was being underestimated by the Obama administration.

Putin, Mattis concluded, was trying to "break NATO apart." Trump has threatened to fire generals who disagree with him, and there's no area where the Pentagon's uniformed brass differ from the president-elect more vividly than on Russia. With Mattis running the Defense Department, those generals will now have one of the loudest defenders imaginable. Whether Mattis goes to bat for them, and how Trump responds, remains to be seen.

On torture

Mattis also opposes torture, which makes him an interesting choice for a president-elect who promised to "bring back waterboarding" and "a hell of a lot worse than waterboarding" during the campaign. In an interview with The New York Times last month, Trump described a meeting with Mattis and said that he was "surprised" and "impressed" by the former general's anti-torture views. This suggests that Mattis may be able to influence Trump away from his stated position on torture, though it does not, as the Times exaggeratedly wrote, mean that Trump has "changed his mind" on the issue.

Mike Pompeo

Pompeo gained exposure to intelligence matters in 2013 when he was appointed to the House Intelligence Committee. In that venue he leveled scathing criticism of the accord. In interviews and written pieces, he has pointed to Iran as the primary source of conflict in the Middle East since Tehran's 1979 revolution.

"Ayatollah Khamenei watches America allow Iran to expand its power while our president writes him missives ensuring we will protect Iran's interests. This is dangerous. The Islamic Republic cannot even feed its own people without access to markets and our president rewards that nation, which has killed countless Americans, with sanctions relief," Pompeo complained in December 2014, before the deal was signed. *"We should make clear that nuclear enrichment is not acceptable inside of Iran for any purpose..."* Last year's deal does allow Iran ongoing limited enrichment.

Earlier this year, after the accord was completed, Pompeo charged that Obama *"has consistently rewarded Iran's depraved behavior, providing billions of dollars in sanctions relief to this fanatical regime through implementation of his dangerous nuclear agreement."*

Pompeo has been one of the leading critics of last year's deal with Iran that traded sanctions relief for a nuclear rollback, aligning him with much of the centrist and right-wing pro-Israel communities. He is a reliable backer of Israel and last November had high praise for Prime Minister Benjamin Netanyahu after they met on an Israel tour.

"Extending sanctions on Iran's weapons programs is an important part of keeping Americans safe," Pompeo said in a statement. *"Re-authorizing existing prohibitions for an additional 10 years provides President-elect Trump and Congress a solid foundation from which to pursue additional action against the Islamic Republic of Iran."*

"While we've had our share of strong differences, I know he's someone who is willing to listen and engage, both key qualities in CIA Director," said Rep. Adam Schiff, D-Calif. on Twitter. The Jewish lawmaker is his party's most senior member on the US House of Representatives Intelligence Committee, where Pompeo also serves

Michael Ledeen

Michael Ledeen is a neoconservative writer at the Foundation for Defense of Democracies (FDD) known for making outlandish claims about Middle East affairs and pushing U.S. overseas military intervention. He has called for waging a global war against "Islamo-fascists," claims that jihadists and Cubans are in an alliance against the United States, and thinks that President Obama supports terrorists. Ledeen, who styles himself a "democratic revolutionary," champions policies that are in line with the Israeli right-wing and is perhaps best known for his hawkish views on Iran.

Ledeen, who was a member of Sen. Ted Cruz's (R-TX) 2016 presidential campaign foreign policy team, has been closely associated with Donald Trump's advisors. In mid-2016, Ledeen published a book with retired Lt. Gen. Michael Flynn, Trump's controversial pick as national security advisor, called *The Field of Fight: How We Can Win the Global War against Radical Islam and Its Allies.*

The book argues that the United States must engage in a multi-generational war against a "formidable" alliance of jihadists and former Cold War foes that may require sending in troops to fight battles across the globe and synchronizing all resources to "similar to the effort during World War II or the Cold War."

The book is vintage Ledeen. For decades, he has pointed to shadowy alliances of terrorists, fascists, and enemy states that are poised to destroy America, penning fear-mongering op-eds and books about "Global Wars" being waged against the United States. In one typical piece he wrote that *"Killing Americans serves several purposes in the war being waged against us (we have yet to seriously engage against our known enemies): first, it's what the war is all about. They want us dead or dominated. Second, it helps recruitment, which had dropped after the defeat of Iran, Syria, and al-Qaeda in Iraq."*

Ledeen was a vocal critic of the Obama administration, frequently accusing President Obama of being anti-American and supporting terrorists. He once told a conservative radio pundit that Obama *"doesn't like America and he doesn't like us."* He added: *"He is a member of the generation that came out of an American school system that teaches our kids that America is the big problem in the world and that we are responsible for most of the world's ills. We have a war to fight and this president isn't going to fight that war. This president is, if anything, on the other side."*

Iran

Iran has long been Ledeen's bête noir, arguing that the country has been heavily involved in supporting attacks against U.S. forces in hotspots across the globe. *"No matter how well we do, no matter how many high-level targets we eliminate, no matter how many cities, towns, and villages we secure, unless we defeat Iran we will always be designing yet another counterinsurgency strategy in yet another place. We are in a big war, and Iran is at the heart of the enemy army."*

Ledeen has also sought to link the Islamic State (or ISIS) with Iran. In an August 2014 piece written for Pajamas Media, Ledeen claimed: *"It seems that Iran gave ISIS support, in keeping with its well-documented practice of supporting all sides in other countries' internal conflicts."* He went on to describe Iran as being in *"cahoots with ISIS,"* whom he described as *"perfect clients"* for the Iranians.

On Iraq and Iran

A longtime Washington insider, Ledeen has held positions (often simultaneously) in media, government, academia, and think tanks since the late 1960s. In March 2003 the Washington Post highlighted his influence within the George W. Bush administration, citing him as one of several elites consulted by powerful White House advisor Karl Rove. The Post reported that, *"The two met after Bush's election. He said, 'Anytime you have a good idea, tell me,'* Ledeen said. Every month or six weeks, Ledeen will offer Rove *'something you should be thinking about.'* More than once, Ledeen has seen his ideas, faxed to Rove, become official policy or rhetoric.

In May 2003, Brown University professor William Beeman drew attention to Ledeen's clout, writing: *"Most Americans have never heard of Michael Ledeen, but if the United States ends up in an extended shooting war throughout the Middle East, it will be largely due to his inspiration. Ledeen's ideas are quoted daily by such figures as Dick Cheney, Donald Rumsfeld and Paul Wolfowitz. His views virtually define the stark departure from American foreign policy philosophy that has characterized United States actions since Sept. 11, 2001. He basically believes that violence in the service of the spread of democracy is America's manifest destiny. Consequently, he has become the philosophical legitimator of the American occupation of Iraq."*

Shortly after the U.S. invasion of Iraq, Ledeen addressed a policy forum hosted by the Likud-aligned Jewish Institute for National Security Affairs (JINSA) in Washington, D.C. Though it was just six weeks since the United States had moved on Iraq, the title of his speech was "Time to Focus on Iran—The Mother of Modern Terrorism." Ledeen said that the U.S. invasion had been the correct move—"*Democracy is the only way the Iraqi people will be able to get back on their feet*"—and told his audience, "*I have never seen a country more ready for democracy than Iran.*" He concluded his talk by reiterating the idea of democracy as a cure-all, saying that, "*the time for diplomacy is at the end; it is time for a free Iran, free Syria and free Lebanon.*"

Ledeen has frequently attacked officials who have attempted to push forward a diplomatic track in Mideast policy. Commenting on Secretary of State Condoleezza Rice's efforts in early 2007 to arrange meetings with Iranian officials, Ledeen opined: "*The delusion that one can settle our little disagreements with the Islamic Republic, if only the right people sit around the right conference table, has seized every administration since Jimmy Carter. Every president has sent emissaries to talk, and every administration has made demarches to Tehran. To date, the net result is hundreds of dead Americans. And yet the delusion persists. Each time it fails, the deep thinkers at Foggy Bottom manage to convince the Secretary of State of the moment that we are just one small concession away from success, and by and large the secretary goes for it, just as Secretary Rice has.*"

In March 2006, Ledeen testified before the House Committee on International Relations, recommending a policy of regime change and revolution in Iran. He argued that the U.S. government has "yet to fight back" against the so-called terror masters there, who he argued "*have waged unholy war against us*" since 1979. "*They created Hezbollah and Islamic Jihad, and they support most all the others, from Hamas and al Qaeda to the Popular Front for the Liberation of Palestine General Command. Iran's proxies range from Shiites to Sunnis to Marxists, all cannon fodder for the overriding objective to dominate or destroy us. ... I am opposed to sanctions; I am generally opposed to military strikes, and I fully endorse support for revolution.*" He added: "*The first step in crafting a suitable policy toward Iran is to abandon the pretense that we can arrive at a negotiated settlement.*"

The Ledeen Doctrine

"While we will have to act against secret terrorist organizations and kamikaze fighters, our ultimate targets are tyrannical regimes. We will require different strategies in each case. We will need one method and set of tools to bring down Saddam Hussein, another strategy to break the Assad family dictatorship in Syria, a very different approach to end the religious tyranny in Iran, and yet another to deal with Saudi Arabia's active support for fundamentalist Islam and the terror network. But the mission is the same in each case: Bring down the terror masters."

For Ledeen, those who oppose his take on Mideast issues are "appeasers," a frequent neoconservative refrain that gained cachet during the late 1960s when Norman Podhoretz, a neocon trailblazer who served as editor of Commentary magazine for several decades, began using the World War II-inspired label to criticize antiwar protestors. Writing in November 2003, Ledeen said that the so-called appeasers in Congress and the State Department *"don't want to know about Iran, because if they did, they would be driven to take actions that they do not want to take. They would have to support democratic revolution in Iran, and they prefer to schmooze with the mullahs."* He concluded: *"I guess some top official will have to die at the hands of (obviously) Iranian-supported terrorists before the Pentagon is permitted to work on the subject."*

In a March 2003 BBC interview, for example, Ledeen claimed: *"As soon as we land in Iraq, we're going to face the whole terrorist network. Iran, Iraq, Syria, and Saudi Arabia are the big four, and then there's Libya. ...You can't solve all problems, I grant that. I mean, I wrote a book about Machiavelli, and I know the struggle against evil is going to go on forever."* Ledeen was referring to his 1999 book on *"why Machiavelli's iron rules are as timely and important today as five centuries ago,"* in which he argued that war *"provides a real test of character"* and *"creates a pool of leaders for the nation."*

Destroying Israel

Wipe Out Tel Aviv

A senior figure in Iran's Revolutionary Guard Corps warned that should Israel launch an attack on his country, Tel Aviv would be destroyed instantly. "If the Zionists were certain that they could win a war against us, they'd have initiated one by now, but since they don't have the strength to do so, they do nothing but threaten," said Mojtaba Zolnour, who represents Supreme Leader Ayatollah Ali Khamenei in the IRGC.

Should Israel nevertheless decide to strike Iran, the Islamic Republic's missiles will fall in the heart of Tel Aviv, "even before the Zionists' missiles will reach us," he claimed, according to Iranian media. Zolnour's comments were reportedly a response to Foreign Minister Avigdor Liberman, that Israel was doing too much talking about Iran's alleged nuclear weapons program, and that "if you want to shoot, shoot, don't talk."

In an implied attack on Prime Minister Benjamin Netanyahu, the Yisrael Beytenu party chief recalled that when prime minister Menachem Begin decided to blow up Saddam Hussein's nuclear reactor at Osirak in 1981, "we woke up the next morning" to hear about it for the first time.

Similarly, in 2007, when Israel allegedly destroyed a Syrian nuclear reactor, "there was no talk about it" ahead of time, he said in an interview with Channel 2 news. Netanyahu has long threatened to attack Iran in order to destroy, or at least hobble, its nuclear program, although such threats have largely tapered off since the West launched nuclear negotiations with Tehran.

Another senior Iranian military official warned that any Israeli attack would unleash a firestorm of missiles on its cities fired by the Islamic Republic's Hezbollah allies in Lebanon.

The Shiite militia has more than 80,000 rockets ready to fire at Tel Aviv and Haifa, said General Yahya Rahim Safavi, military adviser to Iran's supreme leader Ayatollah Ali Khamenei. "Iran, with the help of Hezbollah and its friends, is capable of destroying Tel Aviv and Haifa in case of military aggression on the part of the Zionists," he said, quoted on state television.

"I don't think the Zionists would be so unintelligent as to create a military problem with Iran," the general said. "They know the strength of Iran and

Hezbollah." Israeli military officials meanwhile have tacitly conveyed a threat to the Lebanese group through international media.

New York Times reported, based on maps and aerial photography from IDF officials, that Hezbollah has moved most of its military infrastructure into and around the Shiite villages of southern Lebanon. According to the paper, Israeli officials say Hezbollah's move is tantamount to using the civilians as human shields.

The paper quotes Israeli officials saying the IDF will not be deterred from striking at Hezbollah posts, indicating that the villages would be hit even harder than during the 2006 Second Lebanon War. Hezbollah, meanwhile, is also mired in fights with rebels of nearly every Sunni group opposing Syrian President Bashar Assad, from Islamic State to the relatively moderate militias seeking to remove Assad from power.

A senior IDF intelligence official warned of a heightened threat of conflict over the next two years as a result of "escalation" in the region. In a briefing at the Defense Ministry in Tel Aviv, the official referred specifically to Hezbollah, and to Iran's arming of the group. Israel has repeatedly complained to the UN about Hezbollah's violations of UN Resolution 1701 from 2006, which forbids the group from rearming.

"The Iranian threat is a tangible threat to Israel," said the official, whose country has not ruled out the use of military force to block any attempt by Tehran to produce a nuclear bomb

Hezbollah warfare

Hezbollah evolved as a state-sponsored, distinctly anti-Israeli organization—first as a military instrument of Syria, and then as Iran's strategic asset. When the Palestine Liberation Organization (PLO) was expelled from Jordan in 1971, it moved into Lebanon and spurred the growing Muslim majority to challenge the Maronite Christian government. The Muslim-Christian civil war ensued. Damascus exploited the resulting instability to take military control of Lebanon—which Syria considered its territory—in the hope of threatening Israel on its northern border and retaking the Golan Heights.

Supporting the Christian government, Israel intervened with air attacks in 1976 and, in March 1978, invaded Lebanon to provide a more effective deterrent. Shortly thereafter, Israel withdrew. After four more years of cross-border hostilities, Israel invaded again, this time with some 80,000 troops. Israel quickly routed the PLO and Syrian troops in the southern part of the country, and maintained its presence to deter further PLO and Syrian attacks. In 1983, Hezbollah arose as an anti-Israeli splinter group of Amal, an existing Shi'ite organization. Unable to confront Israel militarily, Syria nurtured Hezbollah, which became the most effective military force against Israel in Lebanon.

Simultaneously, the Shi'ite population was growing. According to estimates—hotly disputed among non-Shi'ite Lebanese parties—Shi'ites constituted 40 percent of Lebanon's population by the late 1990s. Hezbollah increasingly drew the support of Iran, Syria's ally, which enlisted the group as its militant Shi'ite and anti-Israeli proxy in the Arab world. Hezbollah's military effectiveness in drawing Israeli blood eventually afforded it political domination of South Beirut and south Lebanon.

Hezbollah enhanced its appeal by refraining from fighting other Lebanese factions during the civil war, by its incorruptibility, and through charity and community involvement. The organization became the leading proponent of an Islamic republic in Lebanon. As a consequence, despite growing domestic opposition to Hezbollah's armed status, some members of Hezbollah still consider armed hostility toward a common foe—Israel—the linchpin of Lebanon's security, if not its raison d'être.

Hezbollah characterizes Israel's 2000 strategic withdrawal from south Lebanon as a defeat at Hezbollah's hands. Hezbollah Deputy Secretary General Naim Qassem proclaimed: *"We do not need reassurances from anyone on behalf of*

Israel. What reassures us are our arms, our preparedness, and our readiness, and if Israel is planning any action, it knows the level of the response. This is what reassures us and nothing else."

Hezbollah's core comprises several thousand activists, but, as evidenced by its political success, its broader popular support is orders of magnitude higher. Its highest governing body is the 17-member Majlis al-Shura, or Consultative Council, which since 1992 has been led by Secretary-General Hassan Nasrallah. Nasrallah made his revolutionary bones as a Hezbollah guerrilla commander in the 1980s; his religious education and personal charisma elevated him to overall leadership.

Nasrallah is also chairman of the Jihad Council, the organization's military decision-making body, which is one step below the Consultative Council in the organizational hierarchy. Hezbollah's organizational structure is essentially top-down, and its political and military dimensions are unified both structurally and in the person of Nasrallah. Accordingly, Hezbollah is not especially susceptible to deep splits along strategic or tactical lines. The Consultative Council also has formal links to Iran's Supreme Leader (currently Ayatollah Ali Khamenei) and informal ties to the elite Iranian Revolutionary Guards Corps (IRGC).

Hezbollah's domestic political legitimacy, however, rests not only on its Iranian and Syrian connections and its coercive power in the region, but also on its benevolent presence in Lebanon. While generally corrupt and dysfunctional Lebanese governments have been ineffectual welfare providers for decades, an efficient, incorruptible Hezbollah has furnished schools, medical assistance, and food for Lebanese people—mainly Shi'ites—in need.

Although Iran initially subsidized Hezbollah's welfare operations, since the 1990s it has consolidated a domestic support base, placing Hezbollah-flagged charity boxes, depicting cupped hands, in public areas throughout southern Lebanon. If the United States is to launch an effective initiative for demilitarization, it will need to make a compelling case to Hezbollah's constituency as well as the more pragmatic members of its leadership. Even for such improbable efforts, there is hopeful precedent.

Over the past few years, Israel and Hezbollah have both worked to improve their capabilities for the kind of war they expect to fight. And Syria's civil war has changed the strategic landscape greatly.

For its part, Hezbollah has massively expanded the size and range of its rocket and missile inventory. In 2006, it went to war with some 13,000 short- and medium-range rockets, allowing it to strike targets throughout northern Israel. Today it could have over 100,000 rockets and missiles, including a number of long-range systems as well as systems with improved accuracy, allowing it to strike throughout Israel and with increased precision.

Hezbollah is also believed to have made other improvements in its capabilities, including air defense and coastal defense, with systems acquired from or through Syria. It has very likely deepened and improved its anti-armor capabilities with additional anti-tank weapons. And it has improved its defensive layout in southern Lebanon, deeply embedding its offensive and defensive forces in various towns. In addition, the group claims to have developed a capability to undertake offensive ground operations into Israel. According to the director of production for Israeli military intelligence, Hezbollah forces may well penetrate the border and fight within northern Israel in the event of another war.

On January 27 2015, Hezbollah killed two Israeli soldiers in retaliation for the January 18 airstrike against its operatives in Syria, raising the potential for serious conflict to its highest level since the 2006 war. Although both sides are signaling that they are not interested in further escalation at the moment, future exchanges could rapidly devolve into all-out fighting. Furthermore, it is unclear whether Iran -- which lost a prominent general in Israeli strike -- views Hezbollah's response as adequate, and it may yet prod the group toward further action.

Hezbollah's strategic situation has also changed following its commitment of significant forces to Syria, with an estimated 5,000 personnel serving there at any one time. On the one hand, this situation may dilute Hezbollah's interest in serious conflict with Israel, since it limits the number of forces the group could bring to bear. On the other hand, Hezbollah does not appear to have committed the kinds of forces (rocket/missile and antitank) that would be most useful against Israel, and it has gained operational experience in Syria that could make it more effective in a ground war. Moreover, the group could attempt to exploit its new situation by operating through Syrian territory on Israel's Golan front.

The Israel Defense forces have improved their capabilities dramatically since 2006 as well, including enhanced intelligence and strike firepower (air and artillery) that increase their ability to locate and hit targets. They have also enhanced their ground maneuver capabilities by deploying more advanced and capable tanks and armored personnel carriers (the Merkava IV and Namer, respectively) and equipping key armored units with the Trophy self-protection system, which can intercept antitank munitions. Since 2006, IDF ground training has emphasized operations against Hezbollah, though it is unclear how much of this has been done for reserve units.

Israel's ability to defend against Hezbollah's short-to-medium-range rocket threat has also been enhanced through deployment of the Iron Dome system, which did not exist in 2006. And its civil defense system has been upgraded and tested in recent conflicts with Hamas.

In addition to the unique tensions and triggers inherent in the Israel-Hezbollah situation, there are general military advantages to moving up the escalation ladder faster than one's opponent. Doing so allows one to seize the initiative, dictate a conflict's pace and scope, and execute one's plans with fewer restrictions. There is definitely an advantage to being "first with the most." Other factors that could lead to full-scale escalation include the snowballing of violence as each side ups its commitment, an incident that causes unexpected casualties, or domestic pressure to achieve victory.

Against these must be set certain brakes on escalation. For one, neither side can fully ignore its strategic situation, and neither seems eager to risk the extensive casualties and damage that all-out conflict could bring. Hezbollah's Syrian commitment makes it less capable of sustained conflict with Israel, and pressure from allies could steer both parties away from escalation. Whether or not these brakes would be enough to prevent war remains to be seen.

In the event of another large-scale fight, Hezbollah could conduct major offensive and defensive operations. Offensively, the centerpiece of its strategy could be a rocket and missile offensive throughout the depth of Israel. According to Israeli intelligence estimates, Hezbollah would likely attempt to sustain fire of around a thousand rockets and missiles per day, dwarfing the approximate daily rate of 118 achieved in 2006. Perhaps more important, Hezbollah now has missiles with the range and accuracy to strike large strategic targets such as airfields, headquarters, and economically important sites.

An operation of this nature could overwhelm Israel's anti-rocket systems. The weight of the attack would fall on northern and to a lesser extent central Israel, but Hezbollah can now reach targets in the south as well.

The group could also attempt to penetrate Israel via Lebanon or Syria. As mentioned above, Hezbollah has threatened to do so in a future conflict, Israeli intelligence has acknowledged the threat, and the group's operations in Syria have probably given it a better capability to do so. In addition, last year's Gaza war highlighted the threat of offensive cross-border tunneling. While conditions on the Lebanon border are not as suitable for that tactic, Israel is concerned about it and actively searches for tunnels there.

Defensively, Hezbollah would attempt to limit the effectiveness of expected Israeli air operations by dispersing its forces into civilian areas and/or underground, and by using whatever antiaircraft weapons it has, perhaps including new or improved types of surface-to-air missiles. It would also try to blunt any Israeli ground advance into southern Lebanon by relying on its fortified localities there and using antitank and indirect fire systems.

On the other side, Israel could carry out two major offensive operations: An air operation against Hezbollah's rocket/missile forces and infrastructure throughout Lebanon. A large-scale, deep ground operation in which multiple divisions attack the group's ground and rocket/missile forces in southern Lebanon. The inability of airpower alone to negate the enhanced rocket/missile threat would likely make ground operations of some sort necessary.

Defensively, Israel would attempt to use active (Iron Dome and Patriot batteries) and passive (civil defense) measures to reduce the effects of Hezbollah's rocket/missile offensive while waiting for IDF offensive operations to diminish the threat. This would likely mean destroying launch forces throughout Lebanon and seizing launch areas in southern Lebanon. Israel would also have to be prepared to fight on its own soil in the event of a successful penetration.

A general conflict could be expected to produce significant military and civilian casualties on both sides. Fighting on the ground in southern Lebanon and perhaps northern Israel would likely produce the most military casualties. And if civilians were present amid ground operations -- a likelihood in southern Lebanon -- they would suffer significant casualties in those areas. Civilian casualties should also be expected in areas where air and rocket/missile strikes are conducted, especially when defense measures are inadequate.

Damage to civil infrastructure can be expected in both Israel and Lebanon. If Hezbollah can sustain high rates of fire on Israel, some weapons will get through and some targets will be struck, whether through sheer numbers or greater accuracy. And since Hezbollah operates from within civilian areas, Israeli strikes would cause some damage there even when precautions and precision tactics are employed. Lebanese infrastructure such as bridges, roads, and communications facilities would also be targeted because of their military utility.

Such a war would likely cause widespread social and economic disruption in Israel and Lebanon. Hamas was able to achieve this in southern Israel last year, and attacks further north showed the potential for countrywide disruption under sustained rocket fire. Similarly, the 2006 war demonstrated that Israeli air operations could reach deep into Lebanon with significant economic and social impact. A new war would likely bring more widespread air attacks with even broader effects.

Accepting that Hezbollah, like Hamas, cannot be destroyed by military action alone, Israel would likely focus on achieving limited but clear strategic objectives in a new war, such as substantially reducing the group's military capabilities and damaging enough infrastructure to sully its reputation as defender of Lebanon, perhaps increasing public antagonism toward it in the process.

Of course, critics within and outside Israel would protest these objectives for various reasons. And an extended conflict with significant casualties could increase pressure to expand the mission. A major conflict with Hezbollah could also complicate Israel's relations with the United States. If Israel initiates large-scale operations, Obama administration sources might call for restraint, perhaps even painting the action as an effort to collapse the Iranian nuclear negotiations.

A major conflict would also have important implications for the Syria war. Fighting could spread into Syria along the Golan frontier and bring Assad regime forces under Israeli fire. Hezbollah could also be forced to withdraw troops from Syria in order to meet an Israeli offensive in southern Lebanon, weakening the critical support it has provided to Damascus. And if the group suffers major military losses to Israel, its long-term ability to lend such support could be compromised.

Current expectations that Israel and Hezbollah can manage escalation may or may not hold true; similar assessments were made before all of the recent Gaza conflicts (2009, 2012, 2014), and Hezbollah's drastic miscalculation sparked the 2006 war. If a new conflict does in fact break out, Israel and Lebanon are in for a very difficult time. War in 2015 would probably be significantly more intense and destructive than in 2006, and all of Israel would likely be targeted, not just the north. Such a conflict would bring significant pressure to achieve a clear success, further driving the parties to sustain the fighting and raise it to higher levels of violence.

Missiles' Arsenal

Any future war between Israel and Hezbollah will take a devastating toll on civilians due to the Iran-backed terrorist group's practice of embedding its military assets in residential areas.

Hezbollah currently has a stockpile of over 130,000 rockets, more than the combined arsenal of all NATO countries, with the exception of the United States. This number includes long-range rockets and M-600 ballistic missiles, which carry a high payload and would be able to wipe out a good chunk of Times Square and maim and kill people four football fields away from the point of impact. Hezbollah also has approximately 100,000 short-range rockets trained on schools, homes, and hospitals in northern Israel, which could potentially kill hundreds of civilians.

In Hezbollah's arsenal are about 700 long-range, high-payload rockets and missiles with names like Fateh-110 and Scud D. They are capable of taking down entire buildings in Tel Aviv or Jerusalem, wreaking havoc at Israel's major military bases, killing thousands of Israeli civilians, shutting down the nation's airports and ports, and taking out the electric grid. And that's just in the first week.

Former Israel Defense Forces (IDF) major general Yaakov Amidror is talking about the M-600 missile. It's a fairly accurate ballistic missile that weighs more than a Hummer H2 and carries a formidable warhead. The M-600 can also deliver chemical weapons. A single M-600 could wipe out a good chunk of

Times Square and maim and kill people four football fields away from the point of impact. Hezbollah has a lot of M-600s.

Hezbollah's positioning of this weaponry in civilian areas poses a challenge to Israeli officers, added Geoff Corn, an international military law expert at the South Texas College of Law in Houston. "After exhausting all feasible efforts to reduce civilian risk, IDF commanders must resolve the decisive question: Is the potential for civilian harm excessive in comparison to the advantages the attack would provide? When you talk of an M-600 in the hands of an enemy that targets vital military assets or the civilian population—even if that apartment building is full—launching the attack will be necessary to mitigate the threat," he explained.

Israeli military officials in May 2015 told the New York Times that Hezbollah has "moved most of its military infrastructure" in and around Shiite villages, which "amounts to using the civilians as a human shield." One senior military official added that Lebanese civilians are "living in a military compound," noting: "We will hit Hezbollah hard, while making every effort to limit civilian casualties as much as we can...We do not intend to stand by helplessly in the face of rocket attacks."

Israel wants the world to know that a war with Hezbollah in Lebanon will be, unavoidably, awful; and the massive collateral damage won't be -Israel's fault. Even more than that, the IDF seems to be pleading to the international community: Do something. Stop Hezbollah. Before it is too late, and they drag the region into a bloody hellhole.

Yaakov Amidror, Israel's former national security advisor, met with UN Secretary-General Ban Ki-moon in the summer of 2013 and showed him "detailed evidence of Hezbollah's deadly arsenal and the fact that it was strategically placed within densely populated civilian centers." When Amidror asked Ban what the Israelis should do, he "offered no response and no suggestions."

Amidror, Israel's former national security adviser, is asked what the next war between Israel and Hezbollah will look like. "We are not looking for war," says Amidror. "But suppose Hezbollah launches an advanced missile like the M-600 at the Kirya, the IDF military headquarters in Tel Aviv, or a large apartment complex in Jerusalem. Our defense technology quickly finds the launcher. It is right under a 22-story residential building in Beirut. We can now see in real time the launcher being moved back under the building to reload." "We have just minutes to act," explains Amidror. "The IDF will have to take out the launcher because the next missile can cause enormous damage in Israel. But to take out the launcher means the 22-story building may fall. We would try to use precision-guided missiles to protect civilians but the target is hard to reach. We will try to warn the residents but the timing is tight. That building will almost certainly be hit. And the images in the international media will almost certainly be awful."

The international community will look at the images and will note that the immediate cause of destruction was Israeli munitions. But—and here is the kicker—both legally and morally, the cause of these tragic consequences will lie solely at the feet of Hezbollah."

Hezbollah cleverly places its arsenal where any Israeli military response—even legal, carefully planned, narrowly targeted, proportionate measures—will lead to huge civilian casualties among Lebanese. Hassan Nasrallah, Hezbollah's cunning leader, sees a win-win situation. He'd like nothing better than for the IDF to kill Lebanese civilians. When these awful images appear on CNN and the front pages of the New York Times, Nasrallah will paint the IDF as baby-killers and worse.

And if the IDF shies away from attacking legitimate military targets in civilian sectors, then Nasrallah achieves both military and strategic advantages, and his fighters can continue to rain deadly rockets down on Israel's civilians, infrastructure, and military installations.

Hezbollah has amassed not just rockets and missiles. Iran has supplied its favorite terrorist organization with other top-of-the-line weaponry. For military aficionados, these would include the latest guided, tank-piercing Russian-made "Kornet" missiles, SA-17 and SA-22 air defense systems, and even the "Yakhont" class surface-to-ship cruise missiles.

Making matters worse for IDF planners, Hezbollah boasts a standing army of more than 10,000 soldiers—a figure that could add two or three times that amount of reservists in the event of a war with Israel. In short, since its last major conflict with Israel in 2006, Hezbollah has dramatically increased its combat capabilities and armory. The terrorist organization has leapt from the jayvee team to the major leagues across every fighting platform.

True, Hezbollah is stretched these days from rotating its troops into Syria. But that also means that many Hezbollah soldiers will be battle-tested and tough; some 6,000 to 7,000 of them have been fighting alongside Syrian Army regulars in an effort to prop up Bashar al-Assad.

No matter how brave a face the IDF leadership tries to put on, in the next conflict with Hezbollah, IDF tanks will get blown to bits, aircraft will be shot from the sky, navy patrol boats will be sunk, and the multibillion-dollar Israeli offshore gas rigs in the Mediterranean Sea could end up on the sea floor. Many young IDF soldiers will be coming home in body bags. Nothing would make Nasrallah happier. He is clear in public statements that he'd dearly like to murder every Jew in the world but especially those in Israel. In speeches, he describes Israel as a "cancerous entity" of "ultimate evil" and joyfully calls for its "annihilation."

Deterrence is a big part of Israel's defense strategy; acknowledging these scenarios doesn't sit right with many in IDF's military structure. They don't want to frighten Israel's civilian population. Nor do they want to embolden Israel's enemies. But the IDF is trying really hard to give the world a wake-up call about what's coming down the pike.

Even in a best-case scenario for preventing Israel's civilian casualties—meaning a vast majority of Israelis would be able to get into hardened shelters before the first deadly salvo is launched from Lebanon—IDF planners quietly acknowledge that "as many as hundreds" of Israeli noncombatants might be killed per day in the first week or two of the conflict. If Hezbollah's first missile salvos are launched without warning, the Israeli civilian death count could be 10 times higher. We're talking grandparents and toddlers alike.

Israel's top military brass acknowledges that its high-tech missile-defense system will be "lucky" to shoot down 90 percent of incoming rockets, missiles, and mortars. Hezbollah has the capacity to shoot 1,500 missiles per day. That means 150—likely more—deadly projectiles could get through in a day. Israel's Iron Dome, David's Sling, Arrow 3, and other state-of-the-art systems for shooting down incoming rockets and missiles are the best in the world but imperfect. "Even with Israel's technological superiority, it would be a major blunder to underestimate Hezbollah's ability to do serious damage," cautions Amos Harel, the respected military/defense correspondent for the Israeli daily Ha'aretz.

Israel will almost certainly be forced to try to evacuate most citizens in the northern part of the country. Because Hezbollah's arsenal includes about 100,000 short-range rockets aimed at schools, hospitals, and homes. These rockets—including Falaks, Katyushas, Fajr-3s, and 122 Grads—may not be particularly accurate but they're also not in air long enough for the IDF defensive weapons systems to shoot them down.

Imagine if New Jersey shot more than 1,000 deadly rockets over the Hudson River into Manhattan every day. No doubt, those on the Upper West Side would also be a bit peeved. "There is no country in the world—not Israel, not the U.S., not in Europe—who would not go to war to stop a rocket barrage of that nature," explains Nadav Pollak, formerly in an IDF intelligence unit and today a counterterrorism fellow at the Washington Institute.

Small teams of elite Hezbollah commandos will almost certainly be able to slip into Israel and may wreak havoc among Israeli villages in the north. One scenario that has IDF strategists concerned: A Hezbollah team infiltrates into northern Israel via small boat at night, kills every man, woman, and child in a remote village, and then escapes into the darkness. The public relations value to Hezbollah would be enormous. "Anything that creates fear and terror among Israelis is a win for Hezbollah," says an IDF Home Front Command senior official. Another big fear: the kidnapping of IDF soldiers, as has happened before. In fact, it was the kidnapping of two IDF soldiers on a routine patrol along the Lebanese border which triggered the 2006 conflict.

Thumbing its nose at legal and ethical norms for armed conflict, Hezbollah has strategically placed its launchers and other deadly weaponry in homes, schools, hospitals, and densely populated civilian centers throughout Lebanon. This arsenal is supposedly "hidden." Still, the IDF knows where many of these weapons are stored. These maps showed remarkably detailed information indicating that Hezbollah is storing its weaponry in dozens of southern Lebanese villages but also in Beirut proper, where the organization is headquartered in the densely populated suburb of Dahiya.

The IDF is aware that future conflicts with Hezbollah will be fought on at least two battlegrounds. The first, obviously, will involve guns, tanks, and fighter jets. The second front will encompass the court of public opinion. Israel is wisely opening up its second front early. When the next war occurs, the IDF will endeavor to have both law and morality on its side.

"Imagine that you are sitting in Georgetown, overlooking the Potomac River, sipping a great beer, waiting for your shrimp order to arrive," says Brigadier General Mickey Edelstein, commander of the IDF National Training Center for Ground Forces. "Then the alarm sounds, and you have maybe 10 to 20 seconds to get into a shelter. If you are slow, you will be killed. The same goes for your wife, your kids. That's why we will take out Hezbollah's legitimate military targets. Lebanese civilians will need to understand that when Hezbollah uses them as military shields, they are in grave danger."

The IDF no longer distinguishes between the sovereign nation of Lebanon and Hezbollah. Here's why: The terrorist group fully controls southern Lebanon, even to the point of limiting the movements of the Lebanese Army and also of the United Nations forces there. As well, Hezbollah holds significant positions in the Lebanese government and parliament. As such, Lebanon's infrastructure will likely be targeted. The IDF may well go after Lebanese bridges, airports, highways, and the electric grid, and IDF officials want Hezbollah to know this. Again, deterrence.

IDF Air Force lieutenant colonel Nisan Cohen winds back to the scenario of a 22-story building in Beirut with an M-600 launcher in its basement. "Even with our best precision-guided missiles and with our best efforts to avoid civilian casualties," he says, "it's very hard to just hit the basement. It's even harder for us to explain afterwards why civilians were harmed." Cohen knows that the IDF is at a competitive disadvantage in terms of telling its side of the story. Photos of destroyed buildings are dead easy to come by and tug at the emotions, while the IDF often must rely on classified information to explain a specific strike.

"We ask the world not to be fooled by propaganda and by images," says a senior IDF official. "Check the facts. Any reasonable and moral human being will determine that the IDF did the right thing in our targeting decisions. There is just a fundamental disconnect between everyday life and war. If you see a picture of a dead baby, you know that it's bad. You want to blame someone. It's nearly impossible for people to flip that switch and try to understand the legal and factual context of war."

Military minds, of course, know better. In November 2014, the highest-ranking officer in the U.S. military—Martin Dempsey, then-chairman of the Joint Chiefs—said that Israel went to "extraordinary lengths" to limit civilian casualties in its recent war in Gaza and that the Pentagon had sent a working team to Israel to glean what lessons could be learned from that IDF operation. Apparently, the State Department and Bernie Sanders didn't get the memo.

Yaakov Amidror recalls an event from his stint as Israel's national security adviser. In the late summer of 2013, United Nations secretary general Ban Ki-moon paid a visit to Jerusalem. Just prior to a planned meeting with Prime Minister Bibi Netanyahu, Amidror got an hour alone with Ban and his aide-de-camp. Amidror pulled out his laptop and presented detailed evidence of Hezbollah's deadly arsenal and the fact that it was strategically placed within densely populated civilian centers. "What do you want us to do?" asked Amidror. Ban offered no response and no suggestions. Instead, the U.N. chief continued 15 feet down the plush carpeted hallway from Amidror's office to his meeting with Netanyahu.

Deputy Chief of Staff Yair Golan, speaking at a conference today (Monday) shared some projections of what a future conflict in Lebanon would bring to the home front in Israel's heartland. "In the 2nd Lebanon war, 70 tons of explosive warheads hit Israel. Let's estimate the next war will bring four times that and round up. So we're talking about 300 tons per month. That's equal to what our Air Force drops in five hours."

However, Golan argued, the challenge was not insurmountable. "Don't you think we can withstand this? Do we not have a national sense of fortitude?". He also offered statistics that brighten the picture somewhat, "Of all the rockets fired up till now, only 4% have hit in built up areas, and only 1% have hit buildings directly."

Golan was speaking at a conference organized by the National Emergency Management Agency (NEMA), marking the 10-year anniversary of the 2nd Lebanon war. NEMA was created in the wake of the aforementioned war to better coordinate military and civilian action during states of war or national disaster. Attendees at the conference include Amir Peretz, who was Defense Minister during the 2nd Lebanon war, the head of NEMA, the head of the Home Front Command, and other Defence and Emergency Response officials.

According to Golan, "We're the country best equipped to deal with this kind of emergency. I look at the Tel Aviv Metropolitan Area. How many rockets will land there? Several dozens. We can handle that. The Home Front Command has prepared directives for all relevant government bodies, and we just need to make sure that everyone is doing their job and ensuring preparedness. Israel has a peerless early warning system that lets civilians know exactly what to do."

Regarding preparations for dealing with the threat from Hezbollah, Golan said some populations may need to be evacuated from areas adjacent to the border, but made sure to note that he is "opposed in principal to evacuations, despite the fact that some small scale evacuations may be necessary."

Amir Peretz, who served as Defense Minister during the war, also spoke at the conference and warned of the inadequacy of the rocket and bomb shelter infrastructure in the North, saying "It's not good, to put it mildly, and we can't put it on the inhabitants of the North to solve it themselves."

Regarding the lead-up to the war, Peretz said: "Our policy of containment created a perception on the Hezbollah side that we were frozen, and they took full advantage."

Speaking in an interview with Iran's Fars News Agency, Commander of the IRGC's Aerospace Force, Brig-Gen. Amir Ali Hajizadeh said, "Based on our information, Hezbollah's power has so much increased in recent years that they can attack any target in any part of the occupied territories with a high precision capability and with a very low margin of error."

Hajizadeh added that Hezbollah "has always shown that its actions in the battlefield are unexpected and it showed this capability well during the 33-day war (against Israel in summer 2006) and it can make similar moves on any scene today."

The IRGC's website quoted Hajizadeh as saying that Hassan al-Laqqis, the Hezbollah military commander assassinated in Beirut, played a major role in increasing the organizations strike capabilities. Israel has flatly denied Hezbollah claims that it was behind the assassination of Laqqis. Laqqis, who is believed to have commanded Hezbollah troops fighting in Syria's civil war, was shot in the head from close range outside his home in the Hadath district of the Lebanese capital on December 4, 2013. Hezbollah leader Hassan Nasrallah vowed to exact revenge on Israel for the killing of Laqqis.

A RAND study concludes that overall "Hezbollah retains a stronger, more capable, fighting force. While Hamas primarily operates as a traditional insurgency group, Hezbollah can manifest both insurgent-like skills and more-conventional operational and tactical skills."

Hezbollah's military wing, the Islamic Resistance (IR), can be divided into two types of fighters: the so-called "elite," or core fighters—numbering between 300 and 1,000 (perhaps as many as 3,000) and local fighters that can be called to action as needed. The number of local fighters cannot be accurately estimated, because they often include many not formally associated with Hezbollah, but the number may be as high as 10,000. Both Hamas and Hezbollah claim the ability to easily increase its fighting force size—by relying on the willingness of the local population to join the fight.

Hezbollah organizes its fighters into small, self-sufficient teams capable of operating independently and without direction from higher authority for long periods of time. The most significant aspect of Hezbollah's organization is the high degree of autonomy given to junior leaders. This is a function of Iranian doctrinal influences and the entrepreneurial nature of Lebanese society.

Hezbollah's weapons inventory includes massive amounts of artillery rockets (Zelzal-2, the Nazeat, the Fajr-3 and -5, 302-mm, 220-mm, 122-mm, 107-mm); ATGMs (ranging from the AT-14, AT-5, AT-13 METIS-M, AT-3, AT-4, Milan, TOW, RPG-29 and the RPG-7); surface-to-air missiles; and anti-ship missiles.

Hezbollah also posses an unmanned aerial vehicle (UAV) fleet, including 30 Mirsad-1 UAVs from Iran, that gives it an impressive long-range sensor-to-shooter link. Exact numbers are hard to ascertain, but sources believe that Hezbollah has replenished much of pre-2006 munitions inventory since the end of the latest conflict with Israel. The best-known weapon in Hezbollah's inventory is the Katushya rocket, some models of which have a range of 45 miles that has been used repeatedly against Israel.

Prewar estimates indicated that Hezbollah had accumulated up to 12,000 munitions, the vast majority of which were the Katushya. The rockets are notoriously inaccurate, but they served as an area-effect weapon intended to terrorize Israeli citizens and taunt the Israeli military, demonstrating the myth of Israel's military invincibility—Israel's prime strategic asset. Hezbollah enjoys a wider range of weapons than Hamas, notably in terms of more anti-tank weapons, and UAVs.

Both Hamas and Hezbollah are the foremost practitioners and adherents to the military doctrine of Muqawama, or resistance. This doctrine is based on an "ideological view according to which Israel is particularly unable and unwilling to absorb causalities and make sacrifices."

Put simply a war of attrition favors the insurgent Islamists. Unlike Hamas, Hezbollah's recent actions against Israel showed it to be an effective fighting force on many levels. Hezbollah remains the only Arab or Muslim entity to successfully face the Israelis in combat and this provides them with tremendous military cachet.

U.S. Calculations

An armed-and-dangerous Hezbollah clearly is not conducive to stable civil government. Hezbollah's 2006 war with Israel, which resulted from miscalculations by both sides, showed that large weapons stocks outside of the Lebanese government's control, in Hezbollah's hands, only undermine its authority and enrich the conditions for armed conflict. Reports in January of this year that Syria had allowed Hezbollah to use its territory to train in the use of advanced SA-2 surface-to-air missiles prompted warnings from U.S. officials that if Damascus supplied Hezbollah with such missiles, Israel would go to war with Syria. At the very least, as long as it is robustly armed, Hezbollah can indulge the temptation to dominate Lebanon through the threat of force, as it did in May 2008, raising the specter of civil war.

There is at least a limited opportunity for the United States to orchestrate change in Lebanon. Some observers have credited the "Obama effect" with the relative success of the pro-Western March 14 Alliance headed by Saad Hariri—named for the "Cedar Revolution" protests on March 14, 2005 triggered by his father's assassination—against Hezbollah in last June's Lebanese election. While it is unclear that it was in fact decisive, Hezbollah leaders may have made similar assessments. Lebanese who want to see their country normalized—and, therefore,

Hezbollah demilitarized—are perplexed and dismayed by Washington's apparent lack of interest in the issue and don't trust it to prioritize Lebanon's integrity over realpolitik concerns. After the 2006 war, one Lebanese man told journalist Michael Totten, "We love America, but have doubts. They let Syria come in here in 1991 for help in Iraq." The same man rued that "Hezbollah in America is seen as terrorists, I know, but they are a large party in Lebanon and we have to live here with them." For good reason, Lebanese parties are thoroughly intimidated by Hezbollah, and will not push hard for its demilitarization until they are assured of strong and sustained American backing.

In any case, outside powers can no longer contain Hezbollah only by confronting its state supporters, but must also deal with the organization directly—especially if the objective is to shape the environment for eventual disarmament. It is hard to see how this can happen unless the United States follows up on the UK's foray. A diplomatic nod to Hezbollah would serve broader aims of U.S. Middle East policy—namely, rolling back Iranian influence in the region and establishing a regional coalition against Tehran, as well as securing a free and open Lebanon.

To accomplish these goals, it is essential that the United States compete with Iran for influence in Lebanon, and the only credible way to do that is to weigh in decisively in favor of a normalized Lebanese state through sustained, energetic diplomatic activity and an expressed willingness to facilitate demilitarization on the ground. Absent this high level of commitment, any approach to Hezbollah would be seen as mere acknowledgment of its political strength and leave its opposition feeling even more isolated and abandoned than before, and even less inclined to challenge Hezbollah's armed status.

Achieving a stable Lebanon insulated from internal disruption and external threat calls for overt diplomatic contact with Hezbollah in the framework of a policy aimed at eliminating Hezbollah's ability to press its agenda through force both within Lebanon and across the border into Israel. Obama is already committed to re-energizing a paralyzed Arab-Israeli process of reconciliation. Hezbollah's political and potential material support for Hamas significantly inhibits the process. A credible demilitarization framework might at least marginally lower Israel's perceptions of Hezbollah's threat and improve the presently bleak outlook for that process.

Without question, Washington has numerous disincentives to establishing any official contact with Hezbollah, which is, after all, a terrorist group among other things. Obama faces criticism at home for talking to Iran in the wake of the regime's domestic excesses; vitriolic rhetoric about Israel and the Holocaust and accompanying accusations of exposing Israel to a genocidally inclined adversary; and obvious Iranian duplicity on the nuclear issue. The Administration's openness to a rapprochement with Syria is also subject to some doubts.

Scarcely a week after Burns met with Assad, the Syrian leader hosted Iranian President Mahmoud Ahmadinejad and Hezbollah's Nasrallah at a Damascus summit, and thus appeared unlikely to jettison old strategic relationships or to embrace new ones quickly. In addition, the Iraqi government—though apparently with little foundation—has attributed the bombings of the finance and foreign ministries in Baghdad to Syria. Some critics also consider Obama's opposition to Israel's settlements policy to constitute overreaching.

These factors would make any willingness on his part to approach Iran and Syria's most dangerous proxy against Israel open to vituperative debate. If Syria has indeed supplied Scuds to Hezbollah, resort to diplomacy would be greeted by even greater skepticism. Yet these circumstances also argue for bold action, outside the box, so as to break the patterns of internal intimidation and external provocation that have accompanied Hezbollah's political ascendance.

What the United States can do that other parties cannot do—not Saudi Arabia at Taif in 1989, not the UN after Hariri's assassination—is marshal broad domestic and international support for a demilitarization process. While Washington's tactical disincentives to doing so have been noted, it faces no insurmountable strategic barriers. Aside from logistical support for the bombing of the Khobar Towers in 1996 it is believed to have furnished, and suspected training of the Mahdi Army in Iraq several years ago, Hezbollah hasn't conducted hostile operations targeting the United States in a generation. Furthermore, Hezbollah leaders must worry that that Israel will again confront Hezbollah militarily—possibly very soon, other things being equal—in a more tactically measured and strategically sustainable manner, and therefore might conclude that talking about demilitarization would yield Hezbollah some temporary protection.

Nevertheless, given Hezbollah's lethal historical enmity toward the United States, and the reality that it does not crucially need American recognition or support, Washington would have to deal cautiously and circumspectly with Hezbollah. Here the American experience in Northern Ireland offers some qualified lessons. Discreet U.S. political support for Northern Irish nationalists helped solidify Sinn Fein's determination to pursue a non-violent political path. Domestically, President Clinton had to strike a delicate balance between enthusiastic Irish-American politicians and more skeptical players, including the law-enforcement and intelligence communities. Internationally, he had to control the risk of offending the British government and impairing the "special relationship."

The gambit paid off when the IRA announced its unilateral cease-fire in August 1994. Clinton then appointed a prestigious special representative, George Mitchell, to take the lead in framing and shepherding a self-consciously high-profile peace process and lent it political support by, among other things, personally visiting Belfast in November 1995. Granted, when the IRA broke its cease-fire less than three months later by bombing Canary Wharf, and it was revealed to have been planning the operation as Clinton toured Catholic West Belfast, the White House was angry and chagrined.

But Washington did not abandon its support for the peace process. After the IRA reinstated its cease-fire in July 1997, Mitchell's demonstrated even-handedness kept moderate unionists on board. He effectively mediated the multiparty talks that culminated in the Good Friday Agreement and the IRA's agreement in principle to demilitarize.

For Washington to hope for that kind of eventual result in Lebanon, it would have to prepare the ground with Congress as well as with Israel and interested Arab governments, thoroughly explaining its strategy and sequencing and securing cooperation and support. Just as Washington kept London and Dublin well apprised of its moves in Northern Ireland and discussed possible inducements with them, the U.S. government would have to keep the Israeli government and some Arab governments continually informed and broach with them any new security or political arrangements that might be conducive to peace.

In particular, to give Hezbollah's leaders maximum incentive to consider demilitarization, and insure itself as effectively as possible against the potential embarrassment of a Hezbollah backslide to violence, Washington should explore whether Israel would in principle agree to withdraw from the Shebaa Farms—the eight square-mile patch of land on the Lebanon-Syria border claimed by both governments—and refrain from attacking Lebanon in the event that Hezbollah agreed to some degree of demilitarization. The Israeli occupation has provided Hezbollah with a pretext for attacking the IDF and Syria with an excuse for deferring border negotiations with Lebanon.

Thus, an Israeli pullout would remove both a reason for Hezbollah to retain weapons and a source of Syrian diplomatic obstructionism. In addition, the

Obama Administration would have to line up a major-power coalition to support and participate in a new and tough UNIFIL II mission, with a mandate to monitor and interdict cross-border arms traffic. At minimum, the UK, France, Germany, and probably Russia would have to back this initiative.

Bilaterally, U.S military assistance to Lebanon is a valuable carrot. The Bush Administration provided more than $300 million in tactical aid to the Lebanese Armed Forces (LAF) after the Syrian withdrawal in 2005, making Lebanon the second-largest per-capita recipient of U.S. military aid, after Israel. But Washington refrained from furnishing the sorts of strategic weapons—guided rockets, tanks, modern artillery, aircraft, and intelligence-gathering equipment—needed for a robust national defense.

The Obama Administration has essentially maintained the Bush team's position. In 2009, among the equipment the United States provided to the LAF were a dozen unmanned aerial vehicles, some inflatable boats, and a combat-support airplane—in other words, nothing close to real firepower. Such restraint is understandable given Hezbollah's power within Lebanon and the fear that potent weapons could fall into its hands.

Cobra attack helicopters had been tentatively discussed as part of the 2009 U.S. assistance package, but the prospect faded over worries that they would end up being used by Hezbollah. But American restraint on arms transfers also inadvertently strengthens Hezbollah's domestic case for holding on to its weapons by allowing Hezbollah to maintain that, without them, Lebanon's national defense would be insufficient. To dampen this rationale, American policymakers should link the quality and quantity of American assistance to the Lebanese army to strong Lebanese support for an international disarmament effort.

Strategic Communication

At the strategic level, lofty overtures have already been made. Various UNSC resolutions and international agreements, albeit with no current momentum behind them, mandate Hezbollah's disarmament.. The French have led the international charge for following through, and now the British have added their own bilateral efforts. Guarded American participation would make for a full, if largely ad hoc, effort from the three Western permanent members of the Security Council.

Even with that level of great-power backing, though, the idea of disarming Hezbollah still seems risible to many in the Middle East, including some of Hezbollah's once and perhaps future political rivals in Lebanon, such as Druze leader Walid Jumblatt and Free Patriotic Movement head Michel Aoun, both of whom are part of Hezbollah's coalition. But since the Cedar Revolution and the coalescence of the March 14 Alliance, more frequent and energized calls for Hezbollah's disarmament have been heard, especially from Maronite Christian leaders Amin Gemayel and Samir Geagea as well as Hariri. They do not, however, see themselves as strong enough singly or collectively to press the point.

The three powers must not only keep raising the subject of demilitarization within the Lebanese political system, but they also need to prevail on others to do so. Grand demarches notwithstanding, disarmament cannot happen unless public discourse in Lebanon demands it. Accordingly, to prepare the political ground in Lebanon for a major diplomatic initiative, the United States, the United Kingdom, and France will have to mount a concerted effort to convince Lebanese parliamentarians and journalists that they are committed to dealing with the issue of Hezbollah's arsenal and to reassure them that their support remains steadfast. The larger point is that great-power involvement needs to be ongoing and calibrated and not merely sporadic or crisis-driven.

Certainly a U.S. initiative to talk to Hezbollah would be a sensitive and controversial diplomatic effort. In fact, some Lebanese as well as American observers hold that, however imperfect, a relatively stable equilibrium now exists in Lebanon, and that casually considered attempts to change the political dispensation could end up producing disorder and potentially civil war.

To avoid this sort of blowback, the United States would have to acknowledge to Hezbollah that demilitarization could not proceed without Hezbollah's voluntary consent and participation. At the same time, Hezbollah itself would be more inclined to go along with a process involving quiet, negotiated demilitarization than one driven solely or mainly by magisterial pronouncements by outside powers.

Thus, sustained ground-level diplomatic contact would be necessary to give the effort the best chance of succeeding. Obviously, direct contact between senior U.S. officials and, say, Nasrallah or Qassem would confer too much legitimacy on Hezbollah to be diplomatically feasible—even in the supremely unlikely event that such senior Hezbollah figures would agree to meet with Americans.

An appropriate course of action would be for the State Department instead to dispatch mid-level U.S. officials to establish a link with Hezbollah representatives, or possibly for President Obama to appoint a special envoy for this purpose as President Clinton did with respect to Northern Ireland.

Either way, the diplomatic mandate would be to talk to all parties about disarmament and not to have an exclusive dialogue with Hezbollah. To attract the widest international support, however, the Administration should also carry out its approach to Hezbollah openly and unapologetically, and with determination and commitment.

The proposal here is for an elaborate, diplomatically and militarily complex initiative that would derive credibility and momentum from the sustained attention and leadership of the United States and other major powers. It would also expose Lebanese parties to potentially serious near-term risk. Is Lebanon's political integrity worth that risk?

From the moral and political perspective of the Lebanese people, who have still not recovered from an eviscerating civil war that began in 1975 and remain pawns of Iran, Syria, and Hezbollah, the answer must be yes. From the broader geopolitical perspective of the United States and its international partners, in which rolling back Iranian influence in the Middle East and shaping an environment more conducive to Arab-Israeli accommodation are crucial goals, the answer is an even more resounding yes.

IDF alarm

Lieutenant General Benny Gantz said that Hezbollah has become the seventh military power in the world, adding that only the US, Russia, France, Britain, China and 'Israel' possess more fire power than the party.

Speaking at the Herzliya Conference, Gantz pointed out that 'Israel' has to be worried about the military experiences which Hezbollah gained from its intervention in Syria, stressing that the Israeli army has to be alert at the northern borders because Hezbollah fighters still deploy in the area.

The Israeli military chief added that Hezbollah has fought in Syria at several fronts simultaneously, what threatens 'Israel' if the party accumulates and uses all these military capabilities to fight Israel. Gantz considered that the developments in Syria do not serve Israeli interests as long as President Assad rules that country. On Iran, Gantz claimed that using the military power to halt Tehran's nuclear program is "a must".

Israel's Chief of Staff Lieutenant-General Benny Gantz (L) flanked by Israeli Defense Minister Moshe Yaalon in a press conference at the Defence Ministry in Tel Aviv, on March 5, 2014": "The bad news from our point of view, is that while Hezbollah is fighting on three fronts... it is also amassing experience which we will one day face," he added. Gantz warned that in Syria there is "a radical axis developing, led by Iran and Hezbollah. The Lebanese terror organization is up to its neck in everything that is going on in Syria. The global jihad is also gaining strength in that arena," he explained. According to the top officer, Israel would soon "encounter Hezbollah offensives, be it frontally or in the form of widespread combat within Lebanon."

Gantz also expressed concerns over the "dramatic" armament in the Gaza Strip. "We have to maintain our superiority in the sea, on land and in the air, as well as in terms of intelligence" Gantz said. He then turned his attention to Iran, reiterating Israel's mantra on the subject of a nuclear Iran. "Iran has not relinquished its nuclear vision" Gantz stated.

"I am convinced that Iran must be stopped before it achieves nuclear power, which, in turn, will spark an arms race. With the help of the international community, we can make it so that Iran will never get there, be it by use of force or without use of force. Iran must not achieve nuclear power" Gantz concluded.

R&D Master

The improvements in Hezbollah's military and technological capacities can be owed, to an astonishing degree, to the work of one man: Hassan al-Laqis. One of Hezbollah's top innovators and technical minds, al-Laqis was assassinated in Beirut this past December by unknown assailants. While his murderers may remain mysterious, al-Laqis' legacy is clear: Hezbollah is now far ahead of any other terrorist group in the world in terms of the weapons it can deploy, the tactics it uses, and the offensive and defensive technology at its disposal. With the support of Iran, and the guidance of al-Laqis, Hezbollah is not a terrorist group, but rather Tehran's terrorist army.

The higher one goes up Hezbollah's military chain of command, the more secret and mysterious its members and activities become, and al-Laqis was no exception. His work was concealed even from many Hezbollah members, and he was granted relative independence in leading the organization's research and development division. He worked primarily on making Hezbollah's rocket and missile arsenal more accurate and deadly, its internal telecommunications systems more sophisticated and difficult to breach, and, most recently, spearheading efforts to develop Unmanned Aerial Vehicles (UAV), such as drones, for use in both offensive operations and intelligence gathering.

Although al-Laqis' assassination was clearly a setback for Hezbollah, his activities had already made substantial progress at the time of his death, and his life's work will threaten Israel for years to come. Under his supervision, Hezbollah went from being a standard-issue terrorist group employing crude tactics like suicide bombers and katyusha rockets to a technologically advanced paramilitary organization capable of accurately firing missiles at almost any Israeli target, especially civilian areas. The man may be gone, but the fruits of his labors remain.

Indeed, Hezbollah's capabilities have expanded across the board. Its arsenal has grown dramatically since 2006, in both quantity and quality. This includes mortars and small rockets with a range of 24 miles and, more disturbingly, rockets and missiles that can strike anywhere in Israel. Hezbollah is also believed to possess guided missiles accurate to within dozens of meters.

Fighting principles

This style of fighting is based on three principles: Absorption, deterrence, and attrition. Absorption refers to the organization's ability to withstand attack or retaliation. Hezbollah has sought to maximize its absorption capacities by building intricate systems of underground tunnels and bunkers across southern Lebanon, which it uses to store and transfer weapons and fighters from one combat zone to another, and as shelter from IDF retaliation. These bolt-holes also help create the sense of a "disappearing" enemy, difficult to detect and target. After all, you cannot defeat what you cannot see.

Hezbollah also deftly exploits the IDF's rules of engagement, which seek to safeguard civilian lives, by using densely populated urban areas to store and launch rockets. This strategy has a propaganda element as well. Hezbollah is well aware that Israel will be globally condemned if civilians are killed in the crossfire, as they almost inevitably will be given the use of such tactics. While often effective, this tactic is, in essence, a double war crime: Hezbollah fires rockets and missiles directly at Israeli civilians, while using the civilian population it rules as human shields; both of which are entirely illegal under international law.

In regard to deterrence and attrition, both refer to Hezbollah's ability to keep up its fight against Israel without suffering total destruction, thus drawing out the conflict to such an extent that it becomes difficult to bear the cost of sustaining it. Hezbollah's massive arsenal ensures that Israeli towns and civilians will suffer a constant barrage of rockets and missiles, something the director of IDF Intelligence has recently referred to as an "era of fire." In order to destroy this arsenal and the infrastructure used to deploy it, Israel needs a combined air, ground, and sea attack. To be successful, however, Israel will need to overcome Hezbollah's advanced anti-air and anti-ship weapons, countless booby traps and ambushes, abduction attempts, advanced anti-tank missiles, and many other challenges.

In addition, Israel will face intense domestic and international pressure to end the fighting as quickly as possible, while Hezbollah will seek to sustain it in order to inflict maximum damage. The organization has adopted this strategy because it believes that anything short of total military defeat—something that is all but impossible given its strategy of attrition—is a total victory for the organization. They also believe that this will create a sense of frustration and despair among Israelis, giving them the feeling that they cannot defeat such a ruthless, radical, and well-armed enemy.

Revolutionary Guards Corps

The IRGC is generally loyal to Iran's political hardliners and is clearly more politically influential than is Iran's regular military, which is numerically larger, but was held over from the Shah's era. The IRGC's political influence has grown sharply as the regime has relied on it to suppress dissent. Founded by a decree from Ayatollah Khomeini shortly after the victory of the 1978-1979 Islamic Revolution, Iran's Islamic Revolutionary Guards Corps (IRGC) has evolved well beyond its original foundations as an ideological guard for the nascent revolutionary regime … The IRGC's presence is particularly powerful in Iran's highly factionalized political system, in which many senior figures hail from the ranks of the IRGC.

Through its Qods Force (QF), the IRGC has a foreign policy role in exerting influence throughout the region by supporting pro-Iranian movements and leaders. The QF numbers approximately 10,000-15,000 personnel who provide advice, support, and arrange weapons deliveries to pro-Iranian factions or leaders in Lebanon, Iraq, Syria, Persian Gulf states, Gaza/West Bank, Afghanistan, and Central Asia.

IRGC leaders have confirmed the QF is in Syria to assist the regime of Bashar al-Assad against an armed uprising, and it reportedly provided advisers to help the Iraqi government counter an offensive by the Islamic State (also known as ISIS or ISIL) that started in June 2014. The QF commander, Brigadier General Qassem Soleimani reportedly has a direct and independent channel to Khamene'i.

The QF commander during 1988-1995 was Brigadier General Ahmad Vahidi, who served as Defense minister during 2009-2013. He led the QF when it allegedly assisted Lebanese Hezbollah carry out two bombings of Israeli and Jewish targets in Buenos Aires (1992 and 1994) and is wanted by Interpol for a role in the 1994 bombing there. He allegedly recruited Saudi Hezbollah activists later accused of the June 1996 Khobar Towers bombing.

IRGC leadership developments are significant because of the political influence of the IRGC. Mohammad Ali Jafari has been Commander in Chief of the IRGC since September 2007. He is considered a hardliner against political dissent and a close ally of the Supreme Leader. He criticized Rouhani for accepting a phone call from President Obama on September 27, 2013, and has continued to oppose major concessions as part of a permanent nuclear settlement.

The Basij militia reports to the IRGC commander in chief; its leader is Brigadier General Mohammad Reza Naqdi. It operates from thousands of positions in Iran's institutions. Command reshuffles in July 2008 integrated the Basij more closely with provincially based IRGC units and increased the Basij role in internal security. In November 2009, the regime gave the IRGC's intelligence units greater authority, perhaps surpassing those of the Ministry of Intelligence, in monitoring dissent.

The IRGC Navy has responsibility to patrol the Strait of Hormuz and the regular Navy has responsibility for the broader Arabian Sea and Gulf of Oman (deeper waters further off the coast). As noted, the IRGC is also increasingly involved in Iran's economy, acting through a network of contracting businesses it has set up, most notably Ghorb (also called Khatem ol-Anbiya, Persian for "Seal of the Prophet"). Active duty IRGC senior commanders reportedly serve on Ghorb's board of directors and its chief executive, Rostam Ghasemi, served as Oil Minister during 2011-2013. In September 2009, the Guard bought a 50% stake in Iran Telecommunication Company at a cost of $7.8 billion.

The Wall Street Journal reported on May 27, 2014, that Khatam ol-Anbia has $50 billion in contracts with the Iranian government, including in the energy sector but also in port and highway construction. It has as many as 40,000 employees.

Back in 1979

Iran's Revolutionary Guard Corps (IRGC) was founded in the aftermath of the 1979 Islamic Revolution as an ideological custodian charged with defending the Islamic Republic against internal and external threats, but analysts say it has expanded far beyond its original mandate. Today, the IRGC presides over a vast power structure with influence over almost every aspect of Iranian life. Still, some experts say that while the corps is generally loyal to hard-line elements in the regime, it is far from a cohesive unit of like-minded conservatives.

The country's premier security institution of more than one hundred thousand strong, the IRGC fields an army, navy, and air force, while managing Iran's ballistic missile arsenal and irregular warfare operations through its elite Quds Force and proxies such as Hezbollah. It is also one of Iran's most influential economic players, wielding control over strategic industries, commercial services, and black-market enterprises. At the same time, the IRGC often serves as an incubator for senior Iranian public officials, making it especially powerful in the political sphere.

The Islamic Revolutionary Guard Corps was formed by late supreme leader Ayatollah Ruhollah Khomeini in the wake of the 1979 Islamic Revolution that ousted Shah Reza Pahlavi. The IRGC was originally created as a "people's army" similar to the U.S. National Guard; commanders report directly to the supreme leader, Iran's top decision-maker. Iran's president has little influence on their day-to-day operations.

Revolutionary Guards were created as a counterweight to the regular military, and to protect the revolution against a possible coup. In establishing the Guards, Khomeini was seeking to avoid a repeat of a successful 1953 coup that ousted a previous revolutionary government. But the Guards' activities in recent years have been aimed at protecting Iranian interests far beyond Tehran.

Current forces consist of naval, air, and ground components, and total roughly 150,000 fighters. The corps' primary role is internal security, but experts say the force can assist Iran's regular army, which has about 350,000 soldiers, with external defenses. Border skirmishes during the Iran-Iraq War in the 1980s helped transform the Guards into a conventional fighting force organized in a command structure similar to Western armies. The Guards also control Iran's Basij Resistance Force, an all-volunteer paramilitary wing, which, consists of as many as one million conscripts.

International Activities

The Guards began deploying fighters abroad during the Iran-Iraq War (1980-1988), "exporting the ideals of the revolution throughout the Middle East." The Quds Force, a paramilitary arm of the Revolutionary Guard with 10,000 to 15,000 personnel, emerged as the de facto external affairs branch during the corps' expansion. Its mandate was to conduct foreign policy missions—beginning in Iraq's Kurdish region—and forge relationships with Shiite and Kurdish groups. The Quds Force has since supported and armed pro-Iranian militant groups across the Middle East and beyond, including in Lebanon, the Palestinian territories, Iraq, Afghanistan, the Gulf states, and several others, according to the U.S. State Department.

The Guards' alleged involvement in Iraq was a particular point of contention between Washington and Tehran. Former president George W. Bush accused Iran in 2007 of providing roadside bombs to networks inside Iraq. That same year, coalition forces captured several militants in Iraq with alleged links to the Quds Force and Hezbollah. In October 2007, the U.S. Treasury Department designated the Quds Force a terrorist supporter for aiding the Taliban and other terrorist organizations.

In the wake of antigovernment protests throughout the Middle East in 2011, the United States and European Union have accused the Quds Force of providing weapons and other material support to help President Bashar al-Assad suppress the uprising in Syria. In October 2012, a member of the Quds Force pleaded guilty to plotting the assassination of the Saudi ambassador to the United States.

Player at Home

The alleged spread of the Revolutionary Guards' external influence coincides with a growing cachet at home. The Revolutionary Guards are the spine of the current political structure in Iran and a major player in the Iranian economy. The Guards' political influence began its ascendancy as a counterweight to former reformist president Mohammad Khatami. But the number of former Guards entering political life spiked during President Mahmoud Ahmadinejad's first term, beginning in 2005.

Supreme Leader Ali Khamenei has appointed former Revolutionary Guards commanders to top political posts like the presidency (Ahmadinejad) and major institutions, like the Islamic Republic of Iran Broadcasting Corporation (Ezzatollah Zarghami), the Supreme National Security Council (Saeed Jalili), and the Expediency Council (Mohsen Rezaei, a 2009 presidential challenger).

Amid deepening discord between Khamenei and Ahmadinejad in 2011, the IRGC began to target some of the president's allies. The IRGC benefits from the confrontation between Khamenei and Ahmadinejad because it makes Khamenei more dependent on the power and muscle of the IRGC.

Basij Force

Much of the institution's rise to prominence over competing militias and paramilitaries in the post-revolutionary period was due to its effectiveness in suppressing internal dissent. Guardsmen and Basij volunteers have a history of violently crushing riots in Iranian cities, and a unit dedicated to quelling civil unrest, the Ashura Brigades, was established in 1993.

In 2007, the Basij was brought under direct command of the Revolutionary Guards by Major General Mohammad Ali Jafari. The move officially refocused the organization on defending against the type of non-violent "velvet revolution" that ended Communist rule in the former Czechoslovakia.

The reorganization was aimed at quelling the very unrest that surfaced following the June 2009 presidential election, which many say the IRGC helped fix in favor of Ahmadinejad. During protests following the vote, members of the Basij force—dubbed "shadowy vigilantes" by Western news organizations—allegedly beat and killed opposition supporters in Tehran and other Iranian cities.

In June 2011, the United States designated the IRGC and Basij as human rights abusers under U.S. executive order 13533. A March 2013 report by a UN special rapporteur cited "widespread and systemic" torture, harassment, arrest, and attacks against human rights defenders, lawyers, and journalists. Ahead of the 2013 presidential election, opposition activists reported that IRGC forces were once again clamping down on protestors, arresting several people at a rally for Hassan Rouhani, a moderate reformist candidate.

A Money Machine

Political clout and military might are not the only attributes of today's Revolutionary Guard Corps; it is also a major financial player. The Los Angeles Times estimated in 2007 that the group, which was tasked with rebuilding the country after the Iran-Iraq War, now has ties to more than one hundred companies that control roughly $12 billion in construction and engineering capital, laboratories, weapons manufacturers, and companies connected to nuclear technology. IRGC has extended its influence into virtually every sector of the Iranian market. The Guards-controlled engineering firm Khatam al-Anbia, for instance, has been awarded more than 750 government contracts for infrastructure, oil, and gas projects, he says.

Looking Ahead

In recent years, analysts have differed widely on what the future holds for Iran's Revolutionary Guard Corps. Some have suggested the Guards' rising political and economic clout has put it in a position to challenge the clerical establishment. For the past thirty years, the Islamic Republic has been based on a fundamental alliance between the clergy and the Revolutionary Guards, where the clerics have been ruling the country, and the Revolutionary Guards have guarded the Islamic Republic and its values. But now the dynamic has changed to one in which the Revolutionary Guards are both ruling and guarding.

For one, the organization today is factionalized and made up of competing currents. During the Khatami era, for instance, the Guards' leadership supported conservative elements within the Iranian establishment, while the rank and file were more empathetic to the reformists. Under Ahmadinejad, splits emerged most noticeably on economic policy.

In the lead-up to the 2013 presidential election, two top candidates had links to the Guards: Mohammad Bagher Ghalibaf, who led the corps from 1997 to 2000, and Jalili, Iran's chief nuclear negotiator, who is a wounded veteran of the war with Iraq. Many Iran observers see the ascent of these two figures in presidential politics as an affirmation of the IRGC's prominence in Iran's corridors of power.

Missiles and Warheads

Iran has developed some weapons of mass destruction (WMD) programs, and it has a relatively advanced ballistic and cruise missile program. Although Iran is widely believed unlikely to use chemical or biological weapons or to transfer them to its regional proxies or allies, Iran's missiles are considered to pose a realistic and significant threat to U.S. ships, forces, and allies in the Gulf region and beyond. The April 2, 2015, framework nuclear accord makes no reference to limiting Iran's ability to develop ballistic missiles, although the tentative accord indicates that U.S. sanctions on such Iranian efforts would remain in place.

Chemical and Biological Weapons Official U.S. reports and testimony state that Iran maintains the capability to produce chemical warfare (CW) agents and "probably" has the capability to produce some biological warfare agents for offensive purposes, if it made the decision to do so. This raises questions about

Iran's compliance with its obligations under the Chemical Weapons Convention (CWC), which Iran signed on January 13, 1993, and ratified on June 8, 1997.

The Administration asserts that Iran's ballistic missiles and its acquisition of indigenous production of anti-ship cruise missiles (ASCMs) provide capabilities for Iran to project power. DNI Clapper testified in February 2015, that the intelligence community assesses that "Iran's ballistic missiles are inherently capable of delivering WMD."

Tehran views its conventionally armed missiles as an integral part of its strategy to deter—and if necessary retaliate against—forces in the region, including U.S. forces. A particular worry of U.S. commanders remains Iran's inventory of cruise missiles, which can reach U.S. ships in the Gulf quickly after launch. U.S. officials and reports have estimated that Iran is steadily expanding its missile and rocket inventories and has "boosted the lethality and effectiveness of existing systems with accuracy improvements and new sub-munition payloads."

It is unclear the extent to which Iran continues to receive outside assistance for its missile program. Some reports suggest Iranian technicians may have witnessed North Korea's satellite launch in December 2012, which, if true, could support the view that Iran-North Korea missile cooperation is extensive. Table 3 contains some details on Iran's missile programs.

Iran's programs do not appear to have been significantly set back by the November 12, 2011, explosion at a ballistic missile base outside Tehran that destroyed it and killed the base commander.

Iran's Missile Arsenal

Shahab-3 ("Meteor")

The 800-mile range missile is operational, and Defense Department reports indicate Tehran has improved its lethality and effectiveness.

Shahab-3 "Variant" /Sijil/Ashoura

The Sijil, or Ashoura, is a solid fuel Shahab-3 variant with 1,200-1,500-mile range. The April 2012 DOD report indicates the missile is increasing in range, lethality, and accuracy, potentially putting large portions of the Near East and Southeastern Europe in range. In June 2011, Iran unveiled underground missile silos. BM-25 1,500-mile range. In April 2006, Israel's military intelligence chief said that Iran had received a shipment of North Korean-supplied BM-25 missiles, capable of carrying nuclear warheads. The Washington Times appeared to corroborate this reporting in a July 6, 2006, story, which asserted that the North Korean-supplied missile is based on a Soviet-era "SS-N-6" missile.

Press accounts in December 2010 indicated that Iran may have received components but not the entire BM-25 missile from North Korea. U.S. officials have long asserted that Iran might be capable of developing an intercontinental ballistic missile (3,000 mile range) by 2015. That deadline has arrived, and Iran has not announced any tests of a missile of intercontinental range. However, DNI Clapper has testified that Iran has the means and motivation to develop longer range missiles, including ICBMs.

Short Range Ballistic Missiles and Cruise Missiles

Iran is fielding increasingly capable, short range ballistic missiles, according to DOD 2012 and 2014 reports, such as ability to home in on and target ships while the missile is in flight. One version could be a short range ballistic missile named the Qiam, tested in August 2010. Iran has long worked on a 200 mile range "Fateh 110" missile (solid propellant), a version of which is the Khaliji Fars (Persian Gulf) anti-ship ballistic missile that could threaten maritime activity throughout the Persian Gulf. Iran also is able to arm its patrol boats with Chinese-made C-802 anti-ship cruise missiles. Iran also has C-802's and other missiles emplaced along Iran's coast, including the Chinese-made CSSC-2 (Silkworm) and the CSSC-3 (Seersucker). Iran also possesses a few hundred short-range ballistic missiles, including the Shahab-1 (Scud-b), the Shahab-2 (Scud-C), and the Tondar-69 (CSS-8).

Space Vehicle

In February 2009, Iran successfully launched a small, low-earth satellite on a Safir-2 rocket (range about 155 miles). The Pentagon said the launch was "clearly a concern of ours" because "there are dual-use capabilities here which could be applied toward the development of long-range missiles." A larger space vehicle, Simorgh, was displayed in February 2010, and Iran has claimed additional satellite launches since, including the launch and return of a vehicle carrying a small primate in December 2013.

Warheads

Wall Street Journal report of September 14, 2005, said that U.S. intelligence believes Iran is working to adapt the Shahab-3 to deliver a nuclear warhead. Subsequent press reports said that U.S. intelligence captured an Iranian computer in mid-20.

Asymmetric Warfare Capacity

Iran appears to be attempting to compensate for its conventional military weaknesses by developing a significant capacity for "asymmetric warfare" that would maximize Iran's advantages and minimize those of a large, advanced force like that of the United States. The unclassified executive summary of the 2014 Defense Department report on Iran's military capability says that Iran continues to develop "anti-access and area denial" capabilities to control the Strait of Hormuz and its approaches. It is developing increasingly lethal systems such as more advanced naval mines, submarines, coastal defense and anti-ship cruise and ballistic missiles, and attack craft.

The purpose of Iran threatening or trying to block the Strait could be to threaten the world economy, perhaps in order to extract concessions from the international community. It is a long-asserted core U.S. interest to preserve the free flow of oil and freedom of navigation in the Persian Gulf, which is only about 20 miles wide at its narrowest point. The Strait is identified by the Energy Information Administration as a key potential "chokepoint" for the world economy.

Each day, about 17 million barrels of oil flow through the Strait, which is 35% of all seaborne traded oil and 20% of all worldwide traded oil.37 Iran publicly stated that it was stopping or firing on several commercial shipping companies transiting the Strait in May 2015 to force a resolution of commercial disputes with the shipping companies involved, but may have been seeking to demonstrate its potential ability to control the Strait.

Were Iran to take action against the United States and the GCC states, Iranian forces would probably rely most heavily on ships, submarines, and short range missiles. Iran could potentially use its large fleet of small boats to "swarm" U.S. ships. It also has the ability to lay numerous mines in the narrow Strait of Hormuz. Iran has added naval bases along its Gulf coast in recent years, enhancing its ability to threaten shipping in the Strait. In February 2013, Iran began constructing an additional naval base near Iran's border with Pakistan, on the Sea of Oman.

Iran's Conventional Military Arsenal

Military Personnel: 420,000+. Regular army ground force is about 350,000, Revolutionary Guard Corps (IRGC) ground force is about 150,000. IRGC navy is about 20,000 and regular navy is about 18,000. Regular Air Force has about 30,000 personnel and IRGC Air Force is of unknown size – it controls Iran's strategic missile forces.

Security Forces: About 40,000-60,000 law enforcement forces on duty, with another 600,000 Basij (volunteer militia under IRGC control) available for combat or internal security missions.

Tanks: 1,650+ Includes 480 Russian-made T-72

Ships: 100+ (IRGC and regular Navy) Includes 4 Corvette; 18 IRGC-controlled Chinese-made patrol boats, several hundred small boats.) Also has 3 Kilo subs (reg. Navy controlled). 2012 DOD report says Iran may have acquired additional ships and submarines over the past two years, but does not stipulate a supplier, if any.

Midget Subs: Iran has been long said to possess several small subs, possibly purchased assembled or in kit form from North Korea. Iran claimed on November 29, 2007, to have produced a new small sub equipped with sonar-evading technology, and it claimed to deploy four Iranian-made "Ghadir class" subs to the Red Sea in June 2011.

Surface-to-Air Missiles (SAMs): 150+ I-Hawk plus possibly some Stinger

Combat Aircraft: 330+ Includes 25 MiG-29 and 30 Su-24. Still dependent on U.S. F-4's, F-5's and F-14 bought during Shah's era.

Anti-aircraft Missile Systems: Russia delivered to Iran (January 2007) 30 anti-aircraft missile systems (Tor M1), worth over $1 billion. In December 2007, Russia agreed to sell the highly capable S-300 air defense system, which would greatly enhance Iran's air defense capability, at an estimated cost of $800 million. The system would not, according to most experts, technically violate the provisions of U.N. Resolution 1929, because the system is not covered in the U.N. Registry on Conventional Arms. On September 22, 2010, then Russian President Medvedev signed a decree banning the supply of the system to Iran, asserting that its provision to Iran is banned by Resolution 1929. In August 2011, Iran and Russia took their dispute over the non-delivery of the S-300 to the International Court of Justice. After the April 2, 2015, framework nuclear accord, Russian officials indicated they would proceed with the S-300 delivery.

Defense Budget: About 3% of GDP

Al Quds Force

An instrument of Iran's national security policy is not only to deploy conventional force but to supports armed factions in the region, some of which are named as terrorist organizations by the Iran, Gulf Security, and U.S. Policy

Some U.S. observers interpret Iran's objectives in supporting armed factions as attempting to overturn a power structure in the Middle East that Iran asserts favors the United States, Israel, and Sunni Muslim Arab regimes. However, in order not to stoke Sunni-Shiite tensions, Iran often publicly couches its support for Shiite-led movements as support for an "oppressed" underclass. The strategy helps Iran expand its influence with little direct risk, gives Tehran a measure of deniability, and serves as a "force multiplier" that compensates for a relatively weak conventional force.

Some U.S. officials have predicted that, in the event of a U.S.-Iran confrontation, Iran would try to retaliate through terrorist attacks inside the United States or against U.S. embassies and facilities in Europe or the Persian Gulf. Iran could also try to direct anti-U.S. militias in Afghanistan to attack U.S. personnel there. Iran's support for armed factions particularly Lebanese Hezbollah, formed the basis of Iran's addition to the U.S. list of state sponsors of terrorism ("terrorism list") in January 1984.

Some experts speculate that Rouhani seeks to curb Iran's support for militant movements in the region because their activities could injure his goals of broader international engagement.

However, many doubt that Rouhani would be able to do so because he is perceived as having no authority over the Qods Force commander, Qasem Soleimani, who is said to report directly to Khamene'i. Some observers assert that the gains by Sunni rebellions against pro-Iranian governments in Iraq and Syria have cast doubt within Iranian leadership circles about Soleimani's preferred policy of providing unqualified support for pro-Iranian Shiite leaders in the region.

In prior decades, Iran's conduct of international terrorism took the form of assassinating dissidents abroad. In the late 1980s and early 1990s, Iran allegedly was responsible for the assassination of several Iranian dissidents based in Europe, including Iranian Kurdish dissident leader Abdol Rahman Qasemlu, several other Kurdish leaders (including those killed at the Mykonos café in Berlin in September 1992), the brother of PMOI leader Masud Rajavi, and several figures close to the late Shah. In May 2010, France allowed the return to Iran of Vakili Rad, who had been convicted in the 1991 stabbing of the Shah's last prime minister, Shahpour Bakhtiar. Iran has not been accused of dissident assassinations abroad in well over a decade.

Iran is supporting a number of armed factions on several fronts in the region, as well as some regional leaders who the United States has said need to leave office.

Lebanese Hezbollah

Lebanese Hezbollah, which is named by the United States as a Foreign Terrorist Organization (FTO), is Iran's chief protégé movement in the region by virtue of a long relationship that began when Lebanese Shiite clerics of the pro-Iranian Lebanese Da'wa Party began to organize in 1982, after Israel's invasion that year. Iran's political, financial, and military aid to Hezbollah has helped it become a major force in Lebanon's politics, and Iran reportedly was instrumental in persuading Hezbollah leaders to become directly involved in the Syria conflict on behalf of Syrian President Bashar Al Assad.

Recent State Department terrorism reports assert that Iran "has provided hundreds of millions of dollars in support of Hezbollah and has trained thousands of Hezbollah fighters at camps in Iran." Israeli sources report that Iran has given Hezbollah about 100,000 rockets of varying types since the Israel-Hezbollah War in 2006, some of which can reach virtually all parts of Israel.

Hamas

The State Department annual report on terrorism has consistently stated that Iran supplies funding, weapons, and training to Hamas, a Sunni Islamist Palestinian organization which is named as an FTO. Hamas has exercised control in the Gaza Strip since seizing that territory in a civil conflict with the non-Islamist Fatah organization, which dominates the Palestinian Authority based in the West Bank. Hamas opposed the efforts by Assad to defeat the rebellion militarily and a rift opened with Assad and with Iran. Iran has since sought to rebuild the Hamas relationship by reportedly providing missile technology and other equipment.

Iraq

The June 2014 offensive led by the Islamic State organization threatened Iraq's government and Iran responded quickly by supplying IRGC-QF advisers, intelligence drone surveillance, weapons shipments, and other assistance. The IRGC-QF advisers have helped reactivate the Shiite militias as a core of armed support to the faltering Iraq Security Forces.

The United States also supports the Iraqi government but cautions that the government reliance on Shiite militias will hinder efforts at political reconciliation that are needed to defeat the Islamic State in Iraq. The Shiite militias include As'aib Ahl Al Haq (League of the Righteous), Kata'ib Hezbollah (Hezbollah Brigades), and the Mahdi Army of Moqtada Al Sadr (renamed the Peace Brigades in 2014). Kata'ib Hezbollah has been named a Foreign Terrorist Organization (FTO) by the United States.

Syria

In Syria, President Bashar Al Assad has been Iran's closest Arab ally, whereas the United States has called for Assad to leave office. Syria has been the main transit point for Iranian weapons shipments to Hezbollah, and both Iran and Syria have used Hezbollah as leverage against Israel to try to achieve regional and territorial aims. In an effort to prevent Assad's downfall—and the likely accession of a regime run by Sunni Islamists - Iran is providing substantial amounts of material support to the Syrian regime, including funds, weapons, and fighters.

Many accounts indicate that Iran has IRGC-QF personnel to Syria to advise the regime and fight alongside the Syrian military. International and U.S. officials reportedly seek to persuade Iran to abandon Assad, presumably in favor of a figure that Iran would perceive as not inimical to its interests—such as the securing of a weapons supply corridor to Hezbollah.

Houthi

Rebels in Yemen. Iran has been supporting a Zaydi Shiite revivalist movement known as the "Houthis" with unknown quantities of arms and other aid, reportedly including AK-47s, rocket-propelled grenades, and other arms. A senior Iranian official reportedly told journalists in December 2014 that the Qods Force has a "few hundred" personnel in Yemen training Houthi fighters.41 In September 2014, the Houthis seized major locations in the capital, Sanaa, and took control of major government locations in January 2015, forcing Saleh's successor, Abd Rabu Mansur Al Hadi, to flee to Aden.

Some observers have argued that the Houthis' successes—including advancing into Aden by April 2015 despite bombing by a Saudi-led coalition of Arab states—might demonstrate Iran's continuing ability to project influence in the Arabian Peninsula and the broader Middle East. However, others counter that Iran's support for the Houthis does not appear to be nearly as significant as its aid to closer allies like Lebanese Hezbollah.

www.ingramcontent.com/pod-product-compliance
Lightning Source LLC
Chambersburg PA
CBHW051947280526
45789CB00009B/3202